Library of
Davidson College

THE PAGEANT OF MEDIEVAL ENGLAND

Historical and Literary Sources to 1485

EDITED BY
FRANCIS GODWIN JAMES

THE PAGEANT OF MEDIEVAL ENGLAND

THE PAGEANT OF MEDIEVAL ENGLAND

*Historical and Literary Sources
to 1485*

EDITED BY

Francis Godwin James

PELICAN PUBLISHING COMPANY
GRETNA 1975

Copyright © 1975 by Francis Godwin James
All rights reserved
Library of Congress Catalog Card Number: 74-23679
International Standard Book Number: 0-88289-055-7

Printed in the United States of America
Published by Pelican Publishing Company, Inc.
630 Burmaster Street, Gretna, Louisiana 70053
Designed by Barney McKee

Library of Congress Cataloging in Publication Data
James, Francis Godwin, comp.
    The pageant of medieval England.
      1. Great Britain—History—Medieval period, 1066-
1485—Sources. I. Title.
DA170.J35   942

ACKNOWLEDGMENTS

"Bede's Account of the Council of Whitby and of Caedmon." From J. E. King, translator, Bede, *Historical Works*, vols. I and II (London, 1930). Reprinted by permission of the Harvard University Press and the Loeb Classical Library.

"Caedmon's Genesis." From Charles W. Kennedy, *The Caedmon Poems Translated into English Prose* (Routledge & Kegan Paul Ltd., London, 1916). Reprinted by permission, with some abridgment.

"The Battle of Maldon." From Margaret Ashdown, *English and Norse Documents Relating to the Reign of Ethelred the Unready* (Cambridge University Press, 1930). Reprinted by permission.

"Saint Anselm as Monk and Archbishop." First part from R. W. Southern, ed. and transl., *Eadmer's Life of St. Anselm* (Thomas Nelson and Sons, Ltd., London, 1962). Reprinted by permission, with some abridgment. Second part from Geoffrey Bosanquet, ed. and transl., *Eadmer's The History of Recent Events in England* (Barrie and Jenkins Ltd., London, 1964). Reprinted by permission, with some abridgment.

"Jocelin of Brakelond." From *The Chronicle of Jocelin of Brakelond*, transl. and ed. by H. E. Butler (Oxford University Press, New York, 1949). Reprinted by permission of the Clarendon Press, Oxford and the Humanities Press, New York, with some abridgment.

"Richard of Devize's Chronicle." From John T. Appelby, *The Chronicle of Richard of Devizes of the Time of King Richard the First* (Thomas Nelson and Sons, Ltd., London, 1963). Reprinted by permission.

"Roger of Wendover's Account of Bouvines and Magna Carta." From Roger of Wendover, *The Flowers of History*, ed. J. A. Giles (Bohn Library, London, 1849). Reprinted by permission of G. Bell and Sons, London, with some abridgment.

"Two Medieval Romances." From *French Medieval Romances*, ed. and transl. by Eugene Mason (Everyman Library, London, 1911). Reprinted by permission of E. P. Dutton, N.Y., and J. M. Dent and Sons, London.

ACKNOWLEDGMENTS

"Miracles of the Blessed Virgin." From *The Miracles of the Blessed Virgin Mary*, by Johannes Herolt, called "Discipulus" (1435-1440), translated by C. Swinton Bland (Routledge & Kegan Paul Ltd., London, 1928). Reprinted by permission.

"The Mystery of the Redemption." From *Representative Medieval and Tudor Plays*, translated and ed. by Henry W. Wells and Roger S. Loomis (Copyright 1942, Sheed and Ward, London). Reprinted by permission, with some abridgment.

"The Priest and the Mulberries." From *Aucassin and Nicolette and Other Medieval Romances and Legends*, translated with an introduction by Eugene Mason (Everyman Library, London, 1910). Reprinted by permission of E. P. Dutton, N.Y., and J. M. Dent and Sons, London.

"Everyman." From Clarence Griffin Child, transl., *The Second Shepherd's Play, Everyman and Other Plays* (Houghton Mifflin Co., Boston, 1910). Reprinted by permission.

"The Vision of Piers Plowman." From *The Visions of Piers Plowman*, transl. by Nevill Coghill (J. M. Dent & Sons Ltd., London and Oxford University Press, New York, 1945). Reprinted by permission, with some abridgment.

"Froissart's Account of the Peasants' Revolt." From *The Chronicles of England, France and Spain*, by Sir John Froissart, with an introduction by Charles W. Dunn (Copyright 1931, E. P. Dutton Inc.). Reprinted by permission.

"A Chronicle of Henry VI." Partly from *The Brut or the Chronicle of England* (Kegan Paul, Trench, Truebner & Co., London, 1908). Reprinted by permission of Routledge and Kegan Paul Ltd.

Contents

Preface ix

CHAPTER I Anglo-Saxon England 3
Bede's Account of the Council of Whitby and of Caedmon (731) 4
Caedmon's Genesis (ca. 700) 14
The Battle of Maldon (991) 26

CHAPTER II Medieval Monastic Life 35
Saint Anselm as Monk and Archbishop (ca. 1110) 37
Jocelin of Brakelond (ca. 1200) 60

CHAPTER III The Life of the Feudal Aristocracy 81
Richard of Devizes's Chronicle of King Richard the Lionhearted (1190) 83
Roger of Wendover's Account of the Battle of Bouvines and the Signing of Magna Carta (1216) 89
Two Medieval Romances (12th Century) 101

CHAPTER IV Popular Medieval Religion 133
Johannes Herolt's Miracles of the Blessed Virgin Mary (12th to 15th Centuries) 134
The Mystery of the Redemption (14th or 15th Century) 138
The Priest and the Mulberries (13th Century) 149
Everyman (14th or 15th Century) 152

CHAPTER V The Disintegration of Medieval Society 187
The Vision of Piers Plowman (1377) 190
Froissart's Account of the Peasants' Revolt (1410) 202
A Chronicle of Henry VI (ca. 1460) 222

*to the students in the
British History survey at Tulane in appreciation of
their assistance in the selection and
evaluation of these readings*

Preface

The Pageant of Medieval England is unlike any other book of readings now available. It is a collection neither of documents nor of modern interpretive essays. Instead, it is designed to introduce the student to the main currents of British history through sources that combine literary merit, or at least interest, with meaningful historical evidence.

The anthology is intended to meet the needs of the ordinary survey course. Such courses, like most English history texts, deal with the entire medieval period within a relatively short space, stressing institutional, especially constitutional, developments. The selections in this volume illustrate the general aspects of medieval life rather than individual events. To supplement the usual text, they are concerned more with social and religious than constitutional history. Furthermore, since many students lack familiarity with medieval literature and have difficulty understanding the values of the medieval world, the selections tend to be more purely literary and less documentary in character.

The collection has both the limitations and advantages inherent in its approach. Since it is impossible to appreciate the style of an author, or the flavor of his epoch, from a few short snippets, the readings here constitute either literary entities (short plays, stories, poems) or, if only parts of longer works, selections of sufficient length and internal unity to stand by themselves. The choice of a relatively few longer selections has inevitably resulted in an anthology which omits treatment of many important events and movements. Collections of shorter readings can obviously offer more complete coverage. It is hoped that what has been sacrificed in completeness has been more than compensated for in vividness, and that although students may cover less material, they will retain a much clearer memory of what they have read. Each selection is designed to convey a distinct impression, one that will become a clear and recurring image in the reader's mind, rather than part of an indistinguishable mosaic of jumbled recollections.

The anthology provides an introduction to each chapter and explanatory remarks for each selection. References to individual sources, to source collections, and to pertinent secondary works (many of them paperbacks) offer the interested student a guide to additional readings.[1] The editorial comments have been kept brief. The purpose of the book is to encourage each reader to discover for himself the meaning and significance of the readings. The student should, so to speak, treat each author as a witness who supplies historical evidence, whether intentionally or not. Some of the witnesses are none too trustworthy but they all are writing about the world they knew. Thus almost everything they say, or leave unsaid, has historical implications. As the Chinese poet Yuan Mei wrote of an old library:

Draw near! draw near!

Ten thousand yesterdays are gathered here.

---

1. The most valuable single volume providing bibliographical information for the student in British history is Elizabeth Chapin Furber, ed., *Changing Views on British History: Essays on Historical Writing since 1939* (Cambridge, Mass.: Harvard University Press, 1966). An excellent recent period bibliography is Michael

Altschul, *Anglo-Norman England, 1066-1154* (Cambridge: Cambridge University Press, 1969). The most convenient reference for identifying persons mentioned in these readings or in a text is *The Dictionary of National Biography*, ed. Leslie Stephen, 63 vols. (London, 1885-1900).

THE PAGEANT OF MEDIEVAL ENGLAND

CHAPTER I

Anglo-Saxon England

THE GERMANIC INVADERS of the 5th and 6th centuries came close to demolishing Celtic-Roman civilization in southern and eastern Britain. Within two centuries, however, their conversion to Christianity brought them into intimate contact with the classical heritage preserved by the church. The civilization of later Anglo-Saxon England thus represented a synthesis of Germanic and Latin civilization (in itself part Hebraic and Hellenic as well as Roman). One of the most interesting questions is to what degree Christianity altered the basic character of Anglo-Saxon culture. Edward Maslin Hulme wrote that "no permanent change takes place in the religious beliefs and usages of a race which is not in the existing beliefs and usages." [1] It is obvious that the Anglo-Saxons interpreted Christianity in terms of their own experience and traditions; for example, they referred to the apostles as Jesus' thanes. Likewise the Saxon *Wyrd* (Fate) resisted metamorphosis into Divine Providence:

> Many a lonely man at last comes to honor
> Merits God's mercy, though much he endured
> On wintry seas, with woe in his heart
> Dragging his oar through drenching-cold brine
> Homeless and houseless and haunted by *Wyrd* [2]

Nevertheless, Hulme's statement is far too sweeping. The Germanic peoples slowly acquired many new attitudes and values from Christianity. To cite one illustration, the Saxon sanction of vengeance was condemned repeatedly by churchmen, beginning with Theodore of Tarsus, archbishop of Canterbury in the 7th century. The Anglo-Saxon kings supported the church's stand against private vengeance, replacing it by public law. Although as late as the 11th century five men preferred excommunication rather than forego the right to avenge their brother,[3] the older Saxon custom gradually disappeared. The interaction between Germanic and Christian-Roman traditions did not end with the Norman conquest; it remained a persistent theme in English history throughout the Middle Ages.

The first two excerpts in this chapter offer an insight into the character of early Anglo-Saxon Christianity; the final selection illustrates the survival of the warrior ideals of the Germanic invaders five centuries after their arrival in Britain.

Bede's Account of the Council of Whitby and of Caedmon
(731)

The Venerable Bede was born near Jarrow, Northumbria, about 672. When he was only seven, his parents placed him in a monastery at Jarrow which had recently been founded. Here Bede apparently spent almost his entire life, but since the monastery possessed manuscripts brought over from the Continent as well as English manuscripts, he became familiar with the learning of his age. As an author he developed a simple, vigorous style of Latin far superior to that of most of his contemporaries. Bede compiled a general history of mankind in which he divided human history into six ages, the last being that of the period from the birth of Christ to the Day of Judgment. He conceived of his *Ecclesiastical History of the English Nation* as an account of Britain during the sixth age, designed to supplement his commentaries on the New Testament and to show that the age of miracles was not over. Bede completed the *History* in 731. Despite its teleological orientation and the unreliability of many of his sources, Bede proved a painstaking, accurate, and fair-minded historian.

The selections from the *Ecclesiastical History* given below describe the Council of Whitby (664) and the life of Caedmon, one of the earliest Saxon writers.

An Ecclesiastical History of the English Nation
BOOK III/CHAPTER XXV

How the controversy about the time of Easter was moved against those who had come from Scotland [664].

In the meanwhile, after the bishop Aidan was taken from this life, Finan in his room had received the degree of bishop, being ordained and sent of the Scots: who in the isle of Lindisfarne made a church meet for a bishop's see; the which nevertheless after the manner of the Scots he built not of stone but all of sawed oaken timber and thatched it with reed, and afterwards the most reverend archbishop Theodore dedicated it in the honour of the blessed apostle Peter. But the Bishop of the selfsame place, Eadbert, took off the reeds and set to cover it all with plates of lead, that is to say, both the roof and also the walls thereof themselves.

About this time there was raised a hot and constant disputation touching the observance of Easter, they who had come from Kent or from France affirming that the Scots kept the Easter Lord's day contrary to the accustomed manner of the universal Church. Among these there was a very earnest defender of the true Easter, one named Ronan, a Scot born but yet instructed fully in the rule of ecclesiastical truth in the parts of France and Italy; who coupling and disputing with Finan set many aright or inflamed them to a more careful inquiry of the truth: yet was he able in no way to correct Finan; nay, rather he exasperated him by his reproof, being a man of hasty nature, and made him an open adversary of the truth. On the other hand, James, once deacon (as we have shown before) of the venerable archbishop Paulinus, with all whom he was able to instruct in the better way, observed the true and catholic Easter. Eanfled also, the queen, with her train observed after the same manner as she had seen it practised in Kent, having with her a priest of catholic observation out of Kent, by name Romanus: whereby as is said, it happened sometimes in those days that in one year Easter was kept twice, and when the king was breaking his fast and solemnizing the Lord's Easter, then the queen and her company continued yet the fast, and kept the day of palms. Yet this diversity of keeping Easter, as long as Aidan lived, was borne in patience of all men, who had come to know very well, that though he was not able to celebrate Easter contrary to the custom of those who had sent him, yet he set himself diligently to perform works of faith, mercy, and love according to the manner customable with all holy men: upon which consideration he was deservedly beloved of all men, even of those which varied from him about Easter: and was held in reverence not only of the common sort but also of the bishops themselves, Honorius of the men of Kent and Felix of the East English.

But after the death of Finan which came after Aidan, when Colman succeeded to the bishopric, who also himself was sent from Scotland, there arose a sharper disputation about the observance of Easter as well as upon other rules of ecclesiastical life: by occasion whereof this inquiry rightly stirred the minds and hearts of many from fear, lest, having gained the name of Christians, they did run or had run in vain. The dispute reached too to the ears of the princes themselves, to wit of king Oswy and his son Alchfrid; of whom Oswy, being brought up and baptized of the Scots and right skilful also in their tongue, thought nothing better than the manner which they had taught. In his turn Alchfrid, having for his teacher in Christian instruction Wilfrid, a man of great learning (for he had both travelled to Rome on his first visit for the sake of ecclesiastical teaching and spent a long time at Lyons with Dalfinus, archbishop of France, of whom also he had taken the crown of ecclesiastical tonsure), knew that Wilfrid's teaching was rightly to be chosen rather than all the traditions of the Scots: . . . [To end the dispute King Oswy summoned a church council at Whitby.]

And first king Oswy said beforehand by the way of preparation that it behoved those who were united in serving God to keep one rule of living and not to vary in celebrating the heavenly sacraments, who looked all for one kingdom in the heavens; but rather they should search out what was the truer tradition and this should be followed uniformly of everyone: and first he commanded his bishop Colman to declare what his observation was, and from whence he drew the source thereof and whom he followed therein. Then Colman saith: "The Easter which I am accustomed to observe I have received of my elders of whom I was sent hither bishop, and this all our fathers, men beloved of God, are known to have solemnized after the same manner. And this observation, that none may think it a light matter or to be rejected, is the selfsame which the blessed evangelist John, the disciple whom the Lord especially loved, kept, as we read, with all the churches over the which he was head." And when he spake these and such like words the king commanded also Agilbert to declare before them all the manner of his observation, whence it was that it had beginning and by what authority he followed it. Agilbert answered: "Let, I beseech you, my scholar, the priest Wilfrid, speak herein for me, for we both, along with all the other followers after the ecclesiastical tradition, who sit here, are of one mind; beside, he can better and more clearly express our opinion in the very tongue of the English, than I am able to do, using an interpreter." Then Wilfrid, the king commanding him to speak, thus began: "The Easter which we follow we have seen to be kept by all at Rome where the blessed apostles Peter and Paul lived, taught, suffered and were buried: this manner we have noted to be practised of all in Italy, and in France, countries which we have passed through in pursuit of knowledge or desire to pray: this manner we have found to be performed in Africa, Asia, Egypt, Greece and all the world (wherever the Church of Christ hath been spread, throughout different nations and tongues), after one order of time and that without variableness: apart only from these men and them that are partakers of their obstinacy, the Redshanks I mean and the Britons, with whom, being natives of the two farthermost islands of the Ocean sea, and yet not the whole of them neither, these men with fond endeavour do contend against the whole world." . . . [The arguments continue at some length. Colman defends the British tradition by citing many devout men who have followed it, such as Saint Columba. Wilfrid replies by maintaining that regardless the British practices are at variance with the true tradition of the church fathers and church councils.]

Moreover, as touching your father Columba and those which followed him, whose Holiness ye claim to copy and whose rule and commandments ye say that ye follow, as the which have been confirmed by heavenly signs, to this I could have answered, that in the Day of Judgment when many say unto the Lord that they have prophesied and cast out devils and done many wonderful works in His name, the Lord will answer that He never knew them. But God forbid that I should say this of your fathers: for it is much more righteous to think well of such as we know not than to think evil. Wherefore also I deny not that they were servants of God and beloved of God, as the which loved God, though in rude simplicity, yet with a godly intention. Neither do I think that the manner of their observation of Easter is much prejudicial against them, as long as none had come to shew them the decrees of more perfect practice, the which they should follow: of whom I verily believe that had any catholic reckoner then come unto them, they would have followed his admonitions in the same manner in which they are shewn to have followed those commands of God which they knew and had learned. But as for thee and thy companions, if hearing the decrees of the apostolic see, nay, rather of the universal Church and these confirmed by Holy Writ, you scorn to follow them, you sin herein undoubtedly. For though thy fathers were holy men, is yet their fewness proceeding from one corner of the uttermost island of the earth to be put above the universal Church of Christ dispersed throughout the world. And if he be your father Columba (yea, and our father if he was Christ's) was holy and mighty in works, can he by any means be chosen above the most blessed chief of the apostles, to whom our Lord said: "Thou art Peter, and upon this rock I will build my church, and the gates of hell shall not prevail against it, and I will give unto thee the keys of the kingdom of heaven"?

When Wilfrid thus concluded the king said: "Were these things, Colman, indeed spoken to that Peter of our Lord?" And the bishop said: "They were indeed, my lord king." Whereat the king saith: "Can you bring forward any so special authority given your Columba?" Whereon the bishop said: "No." Again the king said: "Whether do ye both agree in this without any question, that these words were principally spoken unto Peter, and that unto him the keys of the kingdom of heaven were given of the Lord?" They answered: "Yea, certainly." Whereon the king thus concluded and said: "And I say unto you that I will not gainsay such a porter as this is; but as I know and have power, I covet in all points to obey his ordinances; lest it may be, when I come to the doors of the kingdom of heaven, I find none to open unto me, having his displeasure who is proved to hold the keys thereof."

When the king so spake, all that sat or stood by, the greater along with them of mean degree, gave their consent thereto; and abandoning their former imperfect usage hastened to change over to those things which they had learned to be better.

BOOK IV/CHAPTER XXIV

How that in the monastery [of Whitby] there was a brother to whom the gift of singing was divinely given.

In the monastery of this abbess there was a certain brother made notable by a grace of God specially given, for that he was wont to make songs fit for religion and godliness; insomuch that, whatsoever of the divine writings he learned by them that expounded them, he set it forth after a little time with poetical language, put together with very great sweetness and pricking of the heart, in his own, that is to say, the English tongue. With those songs the minds of many men were oft inflamed to the contempt of the world and desire of the heavenly life. And indeed others too among the English people after him assayed to make religious poems; but no man could match his cunning. For he himself learned the art of singing without being taught of men nor of men's help; but he received the gift of singing freely by the aid of God. And therefore he could never make any fond or vain poem, but only such as belong to religion befitted his religious mouth. For as long time as he was settled in secular life, until he was well stricken in age, he had at no time learned any songs. And so it was that sometimes at the table, when the company was set to be merry and had agreed that each man should sing in his course, he, when he saw the harp to be coming near him, would rise up at midst of supper and going out get him back to his own house.

And as he did so on a certain time, and leaving the house of feasting had gone out to the stable of the beasts which had been appointed him to look to that night, and there at the fitting hour had bestowed his limbs to rest, there stood by him a certain man in a dream and bade him God speed, and calling him by his name said to him: "Caedmon, sing me something!" Whereupon he answering said: "I know not how to sing; for that too is the matter why I came out from the table to this place apart, because I could not sing." "But yet," quoth he again that spake with him, "thou hast to sing to me." "What," quoth he, "should I sing?" Whereupon the other said, "Sing the beginning of the creatures!" At which answer he began forthwith to sing in praise of God the Creator verses which he had never heard before, of which the sense is this: "Now ought we to praise the Maker of the heavenly kingdom, the power of the Creator and His counsel, the acts of the Father of glory; how He, being God eternal, was the author of all miracles; which first created unto the children of men heaven for the top of their dwelling-place, and thereafter the almighty Keeper of mankind created the earth." This is the sense but not the selfsame order of the words which he sang in his sleep: for songs, be they never so well made, cannot be turned of one tongue into another, word for word, without loss to their grace and worthiness. Now on rising from slumber he remembered still all the things that he had sung in his sleep, and did by and by join thereto in the same measure more words of the song worthy of God.

And coming on the morrow to the town reeve under whom he was, he shewed unto him what gift he had received; and being brought to the abbess, he was commanded in the presence of many learned men to tell his dream and rehearse the song, that it might by the judgment of them all be tried what or whence the thing was which he reported. And it seemed to them all, that a heavenly grace was granted him of the Lord. And they recited unto him the process of a holy story or lesson, bidding him if he could, to turn the same into metre and verse. Whereupon he undertaking so to do went his way, and on the morrow came again and brought the same which they had required of him, made in very good verse. Wherefore by and by the abbess embracing the grace of God in the man, instructed him to forsake the secular habit and take upon him the monastical vow, and when he had so done she placed him in the company of the brethren with all them that were with her, and gave commandment for him to be instructed in the regular course of holy history. But he by thinking again with himself upon all that he could hear and learn, and chewing thereon as a clean beast cheweth the cud, would turn it into very sweet song; and by melodiously singing the same again would make his teachers to become in their turn his hearers. Now he sang of the creation of the world, and beginnings of mankind, and all the story of Genesis, of the going of Israel out of Egypt, and their entering in the land of promise, and of very many other histories of Holy Scripture, of the incarnation of the Lord, of His passion, resurrection and ascension into heaven, of the coming of the Holy Ghost, and the teaching of the apostles. Also he would make many songs of the dread of judgment to come, of the terror of the pains of hell, and of the sweetness of the kingdom of heaven; moreover, many other songs of the divine benefits and judgments, in all which his endeavour was to pull men away from the love of wickedness and stir them up to the love and readiness to do well. For he was a man very devout and humbly obedient to the discipline of the rules; but very zealous and fervently inflamed against them that would do otherwise: wherefore too he closed his life with a goodly end.

For when the hour of his departing was at hand, he was taken before with bodily sickness which was heavy upon him fourteen days; and yet so temperately, that he might all that time both speak and walk. Now there was thereby a building wherein they that were sick, and such as seemed near to die, were wont to be brought. He desired, therefore, him that served him, at the falling of evening on the night that he was to depart from the world, to provide him a place to rest in that building: and the other marvelling why he desired this, when he seemed nothing likely to die yet, nevertheless did as he was bid. And when they were laid in the same place, and were having some merry talking and sporting among themselves and them that were there before, and the season of midnight was now passed, he asked whether they had the sacrament there within. They answered: "What need is there of the sacrament, for your time is not come to die yet, that art so merrily talking with us as a man in good health." "And yet," quoth he again, "do ye bring me hither the sacrament." Which when he had taken in his hand, he asked them whether they were all of a quiet mind toward him, and without complaint of quarrel and bitterness. They answered all that they were very peaceably disposed toward him and were far from all wrath; and they asked him in their turn to have a quiet mind toward them. And he forthwith answered: "I do bear, my dear children, a quiet mind toward all God's servants." And so arming himself with the heavenly voyage-provision he made him ready to enter into the other life; and asked how nigh the hour was at which the brethren should be roused to say their night lauds to the Lord. "It is not far off," answered they. "Well then," quoth he thereat, "let us tarry for that hour." And signing himself with the sign of the holy cross, he laid his head on the bolster, and falling a little in slumber so ended his life in silence. And thus was it brought about that, even as he had served the Lord with a simple and pure mind and peaceful devoutness, so likewise leaving the world with a peaceful death he might come to His sight, and that tongue, which had framed so many wholesome words in the praise of the Creator might also close up its last words in His praise, by the signing of himself and commending his spirit into His hands; and by these things that we have told it appeareth also that he had known beforehand of his departing.

Caedmon's Genesis
(ca. 700)

Unlike most of the Germanic invaders of the Roman Empire, the Anglo-Saxons retained their own vernacular and composed a body of literature in their own language. Nearly all of the surviving manuscripts date from the 10th century and come from Wessex, but the first writings in Anglo-Saxon, or Old English, as modern scholars refer to it, dated from two centuries earlier and came from several regions, including Northumbria. At the opening of the 7th century the Anglo-Saxon conquest of England was virtually complete; by the close of the century the language of the conquerors appears to have been in common use among the population. Caedmon's name is Welsh, yet he spoke English. The religious unity made possible by the Council of Whitby and achieved by Theodore of Tarsus, who became archbishop of Canterbury in 668, helped to establish a degree of cultural uniformity. Although, like Bede, the clergy learned and used Latin, some of them also wrote in the vernacular. Pagan epics like *Beowulf* were written down in a Christianized version. Furthermore, older pagan forms of literary expression were employed in religious writing. Caedmon's hymn to creation, mentioned in Bede's account, may be the first example of such writing. In any event, he was among the first to "apply the Germanic heroic poetic discipline of vocabulary, style and general technique to Christian story and Christian edification," thereby setting "the whole tone and method of subsequent Anglo-Saxon poetry." [4]

The portions of Genesis given below are attributed to Caedmon, who is reputed to have translated that book into the Saxon vernacular. While much of this version probably dates from a little later, it clearly shows the influence of pagan literary forms. It will be readily seen that the Saxon Christians not only put the story of the creation into their own language, but they likewise imposed their own imagery and values upon the Hebraic characters and ideas of the Bible.

Instead of beginning with the creation, like the canonical Book of Genesis, this Saxon version starts with a summons to praise God. It then proceeds with an account of the revolt of the angels, led by Satan, and their expulsion from heaven. This tradition, which Milton later incorporated into *Paradise Lost,* had its origins in certain later apocalyptic Jewish writings such as the *First Book of Enoch* and *The Book of Adam and Eve.*[5] The early church fathers (Basil, Ambrose, Augustine) wrote commentaries on the six days of creation in which they elaborated upon the theme of the revolt of the angels. Anglo-Saxon Christians early became familiar with commentaries and incorporated them into the creation narrative. An explanation of evil as originating with the treachery of Satan toward God fitted in well with Germanic beliefs.

Caedmon's Genesis

Right is it that we praise the King of heaven, the Lord of hosts, and love Him with all our hearts. For He is great in power, the Source of all created things, the Lord Almighty. Never hath He known beginning, neither cometh an end of His eternal glory. Ever in majesty He reigneth over celestial thrones; in righteousness and strength He keepeth the courts of heaven which were established, broad and ample, by the might of God, for angel dwellers, wardens of the soul. The angel legions knew the blessedness of God, celestial joy and bliss. Great was their glory! The mighty spirits magnified their Prince and sang His praise with gladness, serving the Lord of life, exceeding blessed in His splendour. They knew no sin nor any evil; but dwelt in peace for ever with their Lord. They wrought no deed in heaven save right and truth, until the angel prince in pride walked in the ways of error. Then no longer would they work their own advantage, but turned away from the love of God. They boasted greatly, in their banded strength, that they could share with God His glorious dwelling, spacious and heavenly bright. . . .

Fierce of heart, they boasted they would take the kingdom, and easily. But their hope failed them when the Lord, High King of heaven, lifted His hand against their host. The erring spirits, in their sin, might not prevail against the Lord, but God, the Mighty, in His wrath, smote their insolence and broke their pride, bereft these impious souls of victory and power and dominion and glory; despoiled His foes of bliss and peace and joy and radiant grace, and mightily avenged His wrath upon them to their destruction. His heart was hardened against them; with heavy hand He crushed his foes, subdued them to His will, and, in His wrath, drove out the rebels from their ancient home and seats of glory. Our Lord expelled and banished out of heaven the presumptuous angel host. All-wielding God dismissed the faithless horde, a hostile band of woeful spirits, upon a long, long journey. Crushed was their pride, their boasting humbled, their power broken, their glory dimmed. Thenceforth those dusky spirits dwelt in exile. No cause had they to laugh aloud, but, racked with pangs of hell, they suffered pain and woe and tribulation, cloaked with darkness, knowing bitter anguish, a grim requital, because they sought to strive with God.

Then was there calm as formerly in heaven, the kindly ways of peace. The Lord was dear to all, a Prince among His thanes, and glory was renewed of angel legions knowing blessedness with God. The citizens of heaven, the home of glory, dwelt again in concord. Strife was at an end among the angels, discord and dissension when those warring spirits, shorn of light, were hurled from heaven. Behind them stretching wide their mansions lay, crowned with glory, prospering in grace in God's dominion, a sunny, fruitful land empty of dwellers, when the accursed spirits reached their place of exile within Hell's prison-walls.

Then our Lord took counsel in the thoughts of His heart how He might people, with a better host, the great creation, the native seats and gleaming mansions, high in heaven, wherefrom these boastful foes had got them forth. Therefore with mighty power Holy God ordained, beneath the arching heavens, that earth and sky and the far-bounded sea should be established, earth-creatures in the stead of those rebellious foes whom He had cast from heaven.

As yet was nought save shadows of darkness; the spacious earth lay hidden, deep and dim, alien to God, unpeopled and unused. Thereon the Steadfast King looked down and beheld it, a place empty of joy. He saw dim chaos hanging in eternal night, obscure beneath the heavens, desolate and dark, until this world was fashioned by the word of the King of Glory. Here first with mighty power the Everlasting Lord, the Helm of all created things, Almighty King, made earth and heaven, raised up the sky and founded the spacious land. . . .

It did not seem good to the Lord of heaven that Adam should longer be alone as warden and keeper of his new Paradise. Wherefore the King, Almighty God, wrought him a helpmeet; the Author of life made woman and brought her unto the man whom He loved. He took the stuff of Adam's body, and secretly drew forth a rib from his side. He was fast alseep in peaceful slumber; he knew no pain nor any pang; there came no blood from out the wound, but the Lord of angels drew forth from his body a growing rib, and the man was unhurt. Of this God fashioned a lovely maid, breathing into her life and an eternal soul. They were like unto the angels. The bride of Adam . . . was a living spirit. By God's might both were born into the world in the loveliness of youth. They knew no sin nor any evil, but in the hearts of both there burned the love of God.

Then the gracious King, Lord of all human kind, blessed these two, male and female, man and wife, and spake this word:

"Be fruitful and multiply, and fill the green earth with your seed and increase, sons and daughters. And ye shall have dominion over the salt sea, and over all the world. Enjoy the riches of earth, the fish of the sea, and the fowls of the air. To you is given power over the herds which I have hallowed, and the wild beasts, and over all living things that move upon the earth; all living things, which the depths bring forth throughout the sea, shall be subject unto you." . . .

Then God's enemy began to make him ready, equipped in war-gear, with a wily heart. He set his helm of darkness on his head, bound it full hard, and fastened it with clasps. Many a crafty speech he knew, many a crooked word. Upward he beat his way and darted through the doors of hell. He had a ruthless heart. Evil of purpose he circled in the air, cleaving the flame with fiendish craft. He would fain ensnare God's servants unto sin, seduce them and deceive them that they might be displeasing to the Lord. With fiendish craft he took his way until he came on Adam upon earth, the finished handiwork of God, full wisely wrought, and his wife beside him, loveliest of women, performing many a goodly service since the Lord of men appointed them His ministers.

And by them stood two trees laden with fruit and clothed with increase. Almighty God, High King of heaven, had set them there that the mortal sons of men might choose of good and evil, weal and woe. Unlike was their fruit! Of the one tree the fruit was pleasant, fair and winsome, excellent and sweet. That was the tree of life. He might live for ever in the world who ate of that fruit, so that old age pressed not heavily upon him, nor grievous sickness, but he might live his life in happiness for ever, and have the favour of the King of heaven here on earth. And glory was ordained for him in heaven, when he went hence.

The other tree was dark, sunless, and full of shadows: that was the tree of death. Bitter the fruit it bore! And every man must know both good and evil; in this world abased he needs must suffer, in sweat and sorrow, who tasted of the fruit that grew upon that tree. Old age would rob him of his strength and joy and honour, and death take hold upon him. A little time might he enjoy this life, and then seek out the murky realm of flame, and be subject unto fiends. There of all perils are the worst for men for ever. And that the evil one knew well, the wily herald of the fiend who fought with God. He took the form of a serpent, coiled round the tree of death by devil's craft, and plucked the fruit, and turned aside again where he beheld the handiwork of the King of heaven. And the evil one in lying words began to question him:

"Hast thou any longing, Adam, unto God? His service brings me hither from afar. Not long since I was sitting at His side. He sent me forth upon this journey to bid thee eat this fruit. He said thy strength and power would increase, thy mind be mightier, more beautiful thy body, and thy form more fair. He said thou wouldest lack no good thing on earth when thou has won the favour of the King of heaven, served thy Lord with gladness, and deserved His love.

"In the heavenly light I heard Him speaking of thy life, praising thy words and works. Needs must thou do His bidding which His messengers proclaim on earth. Broad-stretching are the green plains of the world, and from the highest realms of the heaven God ruleth all things here below. The Lord of men will not Himself endure the hardship to go upon this journey, but sendeth His ministers to speak with thee. He sendeth tidings unto thee to teach thee wisdom. Do His will with gladness! Take this fruit in thy hand; taste and eat. Thy heart shall grow more roomy and thy form more fair. Almighty God, thy Lord, sendeth this help from heaven."

And Adam, first of men, answered where he stood on earth: "When I heard the Lord, my God, speaking with a mighty voice, He bade me dwell here keeping His commandments, gave me this woman, this lovely maid, bade me take heed and be not tempted to the tree of death and utterly beguiled, and said that he who taketh to his heart one whit of evil shall dwell in blackest hell. Though thou art come with lies and secret wiles, I know not that thou art an angel of the Lord from heaven. Lo! I cannot understand thy precepts, thy words or ways, thy errand or thy sayings. I know what things our Lord commanded when I beheld Him nigh at hand. He bade me heed His word, observe it well, and keep His precepts. Thou are not like to any of His angels that ever I have seen, nor hast thou showed me any token that my Lord hath sent of grace and favour. Therefore I cannot hearken to thy teachings. Get thee hence! I have my faith set firm upon Almighty God, who with His own hands wrought me. From His high throne He giveth all good things, and needeth not to send his ministers."

Then turned the fiend with wrathful heart to where he saw Eve standing on the plains of earth, a winsome maid. And unto her he said, the greatest of all ills thereafter would fall on their descendants in the world:

"I know God's anger will be roused against you, when from this journey through far-stretching space I come again to Him, and bring this message, that ye refuse to do His bidding, as He hath sent commandment hither from the East. He needs must come to speak with you, forsooth, nor may His minister proclaim His mission! Truly I know His wrath will be kindled against you in His heart!

"But if thou, woman, wilt hearken to my words, thou mayest devise good counsel. Bethink thee in thy heart to turn away His vengeance from you both, as I shall show thee. Eat of this fruit! Then shall thine eyes grow keen, and thou shalt see afar through all the world, yea! unto the throne of God, thy Lord, and have His favour. Thou mayest rule the heart of Adam, if thou incline to do it and he doth trust thy words, if thou wilt tell him truly what law thou hast in mind, to keep God's precepts and commandments. His heart will cease from bitter strife and evil answers, as we two tell him for his good. Urge him earnestly to do thy bidding, lest ye be displeasing to the Lord your God. If thou fulfill this undertaking, thou best of women, I will not tell our Lord what evil Adam spake against me, his wicked words accusing me of falsehood, saying that I am eager in transgression, a servant of the Fiend and not God's angel. But I know well the angel race, and the high courts of heaven. Long ages have I served the Lord my God with loyal heart. I am not like a devil."

So he urged with lies and luring wiles, tempting the woman unto sin, until the serpent's counsel worked within her—for God had wrought her soul the weaker—and her heart inclined according to his teaching. Transgressing God's commandment, from the fiend she took the fatal fruit of the tree of death. Never was worse deed wrought for men! Great is the wonder that Eternal God, and Lord, would let so many of His thanes be tricked with lies by one who brought such counsel. She ate the fruit and set at naught the will and word of God.

Then could she see afar by gift of the fiend, whose lies deceived and artfully ensnared her, so that it came to pass the heavens appeared to her more radiant, and the earth and all the world more fair, the great and mighty handiwork of God, though she beheld it not by human wisdom; but eagerly the fiend deceived her soul and gave her vision, that she might see afar across the heavenly kingdom. Then spake the fiend with hostile purpose—and nought of profit did he counsel:

"Now mayest thou behold, most worthy Eve, nor need I tell thee, how fair thy beauty and thy form how changed, since thou didst trust my words and do my bidding. A radiance shineth round about thee, gleaming splendour, which I brought forth from God on high. Thou mayest touch it! Tell Adam what vision thou hast and power by my coming. And even yet, if he will do my bidding with humble heart, I will give him of this light abundantly, as I have given thee, and will not punish his reviling words, though he deserves no mercy for the grievous ill he spake against me. So shall his children live hereafter! When they do evil, they must win God's love, avert his doom, and gain the favour of their Lord for ever!"

Then the lovely maid, fairest of women that ever came into this world, went unto Adam. She was the handiwork of the King of heaven, though tricked with lies and utterly undone, so that through fiendish craft and devil's fraud she needs must be displeasing to the Lord, forfeit God's favour, and lose her glory and her heavenly home. So often evil dwelleth with that man who doth not shun it when he hath the power.

Of the fatal apples some she carried in her hands and some lay on her breast, the fruit of the tree of death whereof the Lord of Lords, the Prince of glory, had forbidden her to eat, saying His servants need not suffer death. The Holy Lord bestowed a heavenly heritage and ample bliss on every race, if they would but forego that fruit alone, that bitter fruit, which the mortal tree brought forth upon its boughs. That was the tree of death which the Lord forbade them!

But the fiend, who hated God, and loathed the King of heaven, deceived with lies Eve's heart and erring wisdom, and she believed his words and did his bidding, and came at least to think his counsels were indeed from God, as he so cunningly had said. He showed to her a token, and gave her promise of good faith and friendly purpose. Then to her lord she said:

"Adam, my lord! This fruit is sweet and pleasing to the heart; this radiant messenger is God's good angel! I know by his attire he is a herald of our Lord, the King of heaven. Better to win his favour than his wrath! If thou to-day hast spoken aught of evil, yet will he still forgive thee, if we will do his will. Of what avail this bitter strife against the herald of thy Lord? We need his favour. For he may plead our cause before Almighty God, the King of heaven.

"I can behold where in the south and east He who shaped the world sits veiled in splendour. I see the angels circling around His throne, in winged flight, unnumbered myriads, clothed in beauty. Who could give me such discernment, except it be sent straight from God, the Lord of heaven? Widely may I hear and widely see through all the world across the broad creation. I hear the hymns of rapture from on high. Radiance blazes on my soul without and within since first I tasted of the fruit. Lo! my good Lord! I bring thee in my hand this fruit, and give thee freely of it. I do believe it is come from God, and brought by His command, as this messenger declared in words of truth. It is not like aught else on earth except, as this herald saith, it cometh straight from God."

Long she pled, and urged him all the day to that dark deed, to disobey their Lord's command. Close stood the evil fiend, inflaming with desire, luring with wiles, and boldly tempting him. The fiend stood near at hand who on that fatal mission had come a long, long way. He planned to hurl men down to utter death, mislead them and deceive them, that they might lose the gift of God, His favour and their heavenly realm. Lo! well the hell-fiend knew they must endure God's anger and the pains of hell, suffer grim misery and woe, since they had broken God's commandment, when with his lying words he tricked the beauteous maid, fairest of women, unto that deed of folly, so that she spake according to his will; and aided her in tempting unto evil the handiwork of God.

Over and over the fairest of women pled with Adam, until she began to incline his heart so that he trusted the command the woman laid upon him. All this she did with good intent, and knew not that so many evils, such grim afflictions, would come upon mankind, when she moved to hearken to the counsels of the evil herald; but she hoped to win God's favour by her words, showing such token and such pledge of truth unto the man, that the mind of Adam was changed within his breast, and his heart began to bend accordingly to her will.

From the woman he took both death and hell, although it did not bear these names, but bore the name of fruit. The sleep of death and fiends' seduction; death and hell and exile and damnation—these were the fatal fruit whereon they feasted. And when the apple worked within him and touched his heart, then laughed aloud the evil-hearted fiend, capered about, and gave thanks to his lord for both:

"Now have I won thy promised favour, and wrought thy will! For many a day to come is man undone, Adam and Eve! God's wrath will be heavy upon them, for they have scorned His precepts and commandments. . . .

"Blithe be thy heart within thy breast! for here to-day are two things come to pass: the sons of men shall lose their heavenly kingdom, and journey unto thee to burn in flame; also heart-sorrow and affliction are visited on God. Whatever death we suffer here is now repaid on Adam in the wrath of God and man's damnation and the pangs of death. Therefore my heart is healed, my soul untrammelled in my breast. All our injuries are now avenged, and all the evil that we long have suffered. Now will I plunge again into the flame, and seek out Satan, where he lieth in hell's shadows, bound with chains."

Then the foul fiend sank downward to the side-flung flames and gates of hell wherein his lord lay bound. But Adam and Eve were wretched in their hearts; sad were the words that passed between them. They feared the anger of the Lord their God; they dreaded the wrath of the King of heaven. They knew that His command was broken.

The woman mourned and wept in sorrow (she had forfeited God's grace and broken His commandment) when she beheld the radiance disappear which he who brought this evil on them had showed her by a faithless token, that they might suffer pangs of hell and untold woe. Wherefore heart-sorrow burned within their breasts. Husband and wife they bowed them down in prayer, beseeching God and calling on the Lord of heaven, and prayed that they might expiate their sin, since they had broken God's commandment. They saw that their bodies were naked. In that land they had as yet no settled home, nor knew they aught of pain or sorrow; but they might have prospered in the land if they had done God's will. Many a rueful word they uttered, husband and wife together. And Adam spake unto Eve and said:

"O Eve! a bitter portion hast thou won us! Dost thou behold the yawning gulf of hell, sunless, insatiate? Thou mayest hear the groans that rise therefrom! The heavenly realm is little like that blaze of fire! Lo! fairest of all lands is this, which we, by God's grace, might have held hadst thou not hearkened unto him who urged this evil, so that we set at naught the word of God, the King of heaven. Now in grief we mourn that evil mission! For God Himself bade us beware of sin and dire disaster. Now thirst and hunger press upon my heart whereof we formerly were ever free. How shall we live or dwell now in this land if the wind blow from the west or east, south or north, if mist arise and showers of hail beat on us from the heavens, and frost cometh, wondrous cold, upon the earth, or, hot in heaven, shineth the burning sun, and we two stand here naked and unclothed? We have no shelter from the weather, nor any store of food. And the Mighty Lord, our God, is angry with us. What shall become of us? Now I repent me that I prayed the God of heaven, the Gracious Lord, and of my lungs He wrought thee for my helpmeet, since thou hast led me unto evil and the anger of my Lord. Well may I repent to all eternity that ever I beheld thee with mine eyes!"

Then spake Eve, the lovely maid, fairest of women. (She was the work of God, though led astray by power of the fiend):

"Well mayest thou upbraid me, my dear Adam! But thou canst not repent one whit more bitterly in thy heart than my heart repenteth."

And Adam answered her: "If I but knew the will of God, the penalty I needs must pay, thou couldest not find one more swift to do it, though the Lord of heaven bade me go forth and walk upon the sea. The ocean-stream could never be so wondrous deep or wide that ever my heart would doubt, but I would go even unto the bottom of the sea, if I might work the will of God. I have no wish for years of manhood in the world now that I have forfeited the favour of my Lord, and lost His grace. But we may not be thus together, naked. Let us go into this grove, and under the shelter of this wood."

And they turned and went weeping into the green wood, and sat them down apart from one another to wait the fate the Lord of heaven should assign them, since they had lost their former state and portion which Almighty God had given them. And they covered their bodies with leaves, and clothed them with foliage of the wood, for they had no garments. And both together bowed in prayer; and every morning they besought Almighty

God, the Gracious Lord, that He would not forget them, but would teach them how to live thenceforward in the light.

The Battle of Maldon (*991*)

The Song of Maldon is a fragment from the late 10th century. In spite of its late date, this epic (written in the vernacular) provides an excellent picture of the heroic ideals of the Anglo-Saxon warrior. It tells the story of a battle fought against the Danes in 991. During a series of raids on the east coast the Danes took possession of an island near Maldon, in the estuary of the Blackwater. Byrhtnoth (earl or ealdorman of Essex) cleverly placed his forces at the end of a causeway giving the only access to the mainland from the island. After an unsuccessful attack, the Danish leader requested the chance to fight on even terms on dry land. Byrhtnoth, with more courage than wisdom, granted his wish, thereby helping to bring about his own defeat. After their victory in Essex the Danes raided Kent, Hampshire, and Wessex, demanding and receiving tribute (Danegeld) before they would depart.[6]

Anglo-Saxon society had a military base. The kings were primarily military commanders, the aristocracy comprised the officer class, and the freemen represented the bulk of the fighting force. There is some disagreement concerning the relative importance of these elements, especially after the Saxons became permanently settled in Britain. Older historians, relying on Roman commentators on the Germans, such as Tacitus, saw Anglo-Saxon England as a society of free villagers ruled over by a limited aristocracy and an elected king. In contrast, many modern scholars, depending upon such sources as Bede and *Beowulf,* stress the predominant importance of the territorial rulers (kings and ealdormen) and their band of retainers, or *comitatus*.[7] One thing is clear: the ideals of courage and personal loyalty associated with the *comitatus* still made a strong appeal to the Anglo-Saxon imagination in the 11th century.

According to C. Warren Hollister, the fighting men led by Byrhtnoth at Maldon consisted both of his retainers, drawn from the landed warrior class of thanes, and of well-armed peasants. These latter, he believes, represented not the general militia or *fyrd* but a select *fyrd* based on military obligation owed by all freemen who possessed five hides of land.[8] By the 10th century the ordinary peasant, even if still free, and many had become serfs, did not normally fight.

The battle of Maldon took place during the Danish attacks of Ethelred's reign (978-1016), which preceded Sweyn's invasion in 1013. King Ethelred the Unready (or without council) was much criticized for his weakness toward the invaders, but it appears that the Danes held him in respect and avoided open combat with the Saxons whenever possible.[9]

The Battle of Maldon

Then he bade each warrior leave his horse, drive it afar and go forth on foot, and trust to his hands and to his good intent.

Then Offa's kinsman first perceived that the earl would suffer no faintness of heart; he let his loved hawk fly from his hand to the wood and advanced to the fight. By this it might be seen that the lad would not waver in the strife now that he had taken up his arms.

With him Eadric would help his lord, his chief in the fray. He advanced to war with spear in hand; as long as he might grasp his shield and broad sword, he kept his purpose firm. He made good his vow, now that the time had come for him to fight before his lord.

Then Byrhtnoth began to array his men; he rode and gave

counsel and taught his warriors how they should stand and keep their ground, bade them hold their shields aright, firm with their hands and fear not at all. When he had meetly arrayed his host, he alighted among the people where it pleased him best, where he knew his body-guard to be most loyal.

Then the messenger of the Vikings stood on the bank, he called sternly, uttered words, boastfully speaking the seafarers' message to the earl, as he stood on the shore. "Bold seamen have sent me to you, and bade me say, that it is for you to send treasure quickly in return for peace, and it will be better for you all that you buy off an attack with tribute, rather than that men so fierce as we should give you battle. There is no need that we destroy each other, if you are rich enough for this. In return for the gold we are ready to make a truce with you. If you who are richest determine to redeem your people, and to give to the seamen on their own terms wealth to win their friendship and make peace with us, we will betake us to our ships with the treasure, put to sea and keep faith with you."

Byrhtnoth lifted up his voice, grasped his shield and shook his supple spear, gave forth words, angry and resolute, and made him answer: "Hear you, searover, what this folk says? For tribute they will give you spears, poisoned point and ancient sword, such war gear as will profit you little in the battle. Messenger of the seamen, take back a message say to your people a far less pleasing tale, how that there stands here with his troop an earl of unstained renown, who is ready to guard this realm, the home of Ethelred my lord, people and land; it is the heathen that shall fall in the battle. It seems to me too poor a thing that you should go with our treasure unfought to your ships, now that you have made your way thus far into our land. Not so easily shall you win tribute; peace must be made with point and edge, with grim battle-play, before we give tribute."

Then he bade his warriors advance, bearing their shields, until they all stood on the river bank. Because of the water neither host might come to the other. There came the tide, flowing in after the ebb; the currents met and joined. All too long it seemed before they might clash their spears together. Thus in noble array they stood about Pante's stream, the flower of the East Saxons and the shipmen's host. None of them might harm another, unless a man should meet his death through a javelin's flight.

The tide went out, the seamen stood ready, many a Viking eager for war. Then the bulwark of heroes appointed a warrior, handy in war, to hold the bridge, Wulfstan was his name, accounted valiant among his kin. It was he Ceaola's son, who with his javelin shot down the first man that was so hardy as to set foot upon the bridge. There with Wulfstan stood warriors unafraid, AElfhere and Maccus, a dauntless pair; they had no thought of flight at the ford, but warded themselves stoutly against the foe, as long as they might wield their weapons. When the Vikings knew and saw full well that they had to deal with grim defenders of the bridge, the hateful strangers betook themselves to guile, craved leave to land, to pass over the ford and lead their men across. Then the earl, in his pride, began to give ground all too much to the hateful folk; Byrhthelm's son called over the cold water (the warriors gave ear): "Now is the way open before you; come quickly, men, to meet us in battle, God alone knows to whom it shall fall to hold the field."

The wolves of slaughter pressed forward, they recked not for the water, that Viking host; west over Pante, over the gleaming water they came with their bucklers, the seamen came to land with their linden shields.

There, ready to meet the foe, stood Byrhtnoth and his men. He bade them form the war-hedge with their shields, and hold their rank stoutly against the foe. The battle was now at hand, and the glory that comes in strife. Now was the time when those who were doomed should fall. Clamour arose; ravens went circling, the eagle greedy for carrion. There was a cry upon earth.

They let the spears, hard as files, fly from their hands, well-ground javelins. Bows were busy, point pierced shield; fierce was the rush of battle, warriors fell on either hand, men lay dead.

Wulfmaer was wounded, he took his place among the slain; Byrhtnoth's kinsman, his sister's son, was cruelly cut down with swords. Then was payment given to the Vikings; I heard that Edward smote one fiercely with his blade, and spared not his stroke, so that the doomed warrior fell at his feet. For this his lord gave his chamberlain thanks when time allowed.

Thus the stout-hearted warriors held their ground in the fray. Eagerly they strove, those men at arms, who might be the first to take with his spear the life of some doomed man. The slain fell to the earth.

The men stood firm; Byrhtnoth exhorted them, bade each warrior, who would win glory in fight against the Danes, to give his mind to war.

Then came one, strong in battle; he raised his weapon, his shield to defend him and bore down upon the man; the earl, no less resolute, advanced against the "churl." Each had evil intent toward the other. Then the pirate sent a southern spear, so that the lord of warriors was stricken. He pushed with his shield so that the shaft was splintered, and shivered the spear so that it sprang back again. The warrior was enraged; he pierced with his lance the proud Viking who had given him the wound. The warrior was deft; he drove his spear through the young man's neck; his hand guided it so that it took the life of his deadly foe. Quickly he shot down another, so that his corselet burst asunder; he was wounded through his mail in the breast, a poisoned point pierced his heart. The earl was more content; then the proud man laughed, and gave thanks to his Creator for the day's work that the Lord had granted him.

Then one of the warriors let a dart fly from his hand, so that it pierced all too deeply Ethelred's noble thane. By his side stood a warrior not full grown, a boy in war. Right boldly he drew from the warrior the bloody spear, Wulfstan's son, Wulfmaer the young, and let the weapon, wondrous strong, speed back again; the point drove in so that he who had so cruelly pierced his lord lay dead on the ground. Then a man, ill armed, approached the earl, with intent to bear off the warrior's treasure, his raiment and his rings and his well-decked sword. Then Byrhtnoth drew his blade, broad and of burnished edge, and smote upon his mail. All too quickly one of the seamen checked his hand, crippling the arm of the earl. Then his golden-hilted sword fell to the earth; he could not use his hard blade nor wield a weapon. Yet still the white-haired warrior spoke as before, emboldened his men and bade the heroes press on. He could no longer now stand firm on his feet. The earl looked up to heaven and cried aloud: "I thank thee, Ruler of Nations, for all the joys that I have met with in this world. Now I have most need, gracious Creator, that thou grant my spirit grace, that my soul fare to thee, into thy keeping, Lord of Angels, and pass in peace. It is my prayer to thee that fiends of hell may not entreat [treat] it shamefully."

Then the heathen wretches cut him down, and both the warriors who stood near by, AElfnoth and Wulfmaer, lay overthrown; they yielded their lives at their lord's side.

Then those who had no wish to be there turned from the battle. Odda's sons were first in the flight; Godric for one turned his back on war, forsook the hero who had given him many a steed. He leapt upon the horse that had been his lord's, on the trappings to which he had no right. With him his brothers both galloped away. Godwin and Godwig, they had no taste for war, but turned from the battle and made for the wood, fled to the fastness and saved their lives, and more men than was fitting at all, if they had but remembered all the favours that he had done them for their good. It was as Offa had told them on the field when he held a council, that many were speaking proudly there, who later would not stand firm in time of need.

Now was fallen the people's chief, Ethelred's earl. All the retainers saw how their lord lay dead. Then the proud thanes pressed on, hastened eagerly, those undaunted men. All desired one of two things, to lose their lives or to avenge the one they loved.

With these words, AElfric's son urged them to go forth, a warrior young in years, he lifted up his voice and spoke with courage. AElfwine said: "Remember the words that we uttered many a time over the mead, when on the bench, heroes in hall, we made our boast about hard strife. Now it may be proved which of us is bold! I will make known my lineage to all, how I was born in Mercia of a great race. Ealhelm was my grandfather called, a wise ealdorman, happy in this world's goods. Thanes shall have no cause to reproach me among my people that I was ready to forsake this action, and seek my home, now that my lord lies low, but down in battle. This is no common grief to me, he was both my kinsman and my lord."

Then he advanced (his mind was set on revenge), till he pierced with his lance a seaman from among the host, so that the man lay on the earth, borne down with his weapon.

Then Offa began to exhort his comrades, his friends and companions, that they should press on. He lifted up his voice and shook his ash-wood spear: "Lo, AElfwine, you have exhorted all us thanes in time of need. Now that our lord lies low, the earl on the ground, it is needful for us all that each warrior embolden the other to war, as long as he can keep and hold his weapon, hard blade, spear and trusty sword. Godric, Odda's cowardly son, has betrayed us all. Too many a man, when he rode on that horse, on that proud steed, deemed that it was our lord. So was our host divided on the field, the shield-wall broken. A curse upon his deed, in that he has put so many a man to flight!"

Leofsunu lifted up his voice and raised his shield, his buckler to defend him, and gave him this answer: "This I avow, that I will not flee a foot-space hence, but will press on and avenge my liege lord in the flight. About Sturmer the steadfast heroes will have no need to reproach me now that my lord has fallen, that I made my way home, and turned from the battle, a lordless man. Rather shall weapon, spear-point and iron blade, be my end." He pressed on wrathful and fought sternly, despising flight.

Dunhere spoke and shook his lance; a simple churl, he cried above them all, and bade each warrior avenge Byrhtnoth: "He that thinks to avenge his lord, his chief in the press, may not waver nor reck for his life." Then they went forth, and took no thought for life; the retainers began to fight hardily, those fierce warriors. They prayed God that they might take vengeance for their lord, and work slaughter among their foes.

The hostage began to help them eagerly; he came of a stout Northumbrian kin, Aescferth was his name, Ecglaf's son. He did not flinch in the war-play, but urged forth the dart unceasingly. Now he shot upon a shield, now he hit his man; ever he dealt out wounds, as long as he could wield his weapons.

Still in the van stood Edward the Long, bold and eager; he spoke vaunting words, how that he would not flee a foot-space or turn back, now that his lord lay dead. He broke the shield and fought against the warriors, until he had taken due vengeance upon the seamen for his lord. Then he himself lay among the slain.

So too did AEthelric, Sibyrht's brother, a noble companion, eager and impetuous, he fought right fiercely, and many another. They clove the hollow shield and defended themselves boldly. The buckler's edge burst and the corselet sang a fearful song.

Then Offa smote a seaman in the fight, so that he fell to the earth. Gadd's kinsman too was brought to the ground, Offa himself was quickly cut to pieces in the fray. Yet he had compassed what he had promised his chief, as he bandied vows with his generous lord in days gone by, that they should both ride home to the town unhurt or fall among the host, perish of wounds on the field. He lay, as befits a thane, at his lord's side.

Then came a crashing of shields; seamen pressed on, enraged by war; the spear oft pierced the life-house of the doomed. Wistan went forth, Thurstan's son, and fought against the men. Wighelm's child was the death of three in the press, before he himself lay among the slain.

That was a fierce encounter; warriors stood firm in the strife.

Men were falling, worn out with their wounds; the slain fell to the earth.

Oswald and Eadwold all the while, that pair of brothers, urged on the men, prayed their dear kinsmen to stand firm in the hour of need, and use their weapons in no weak fashion.

Byrhtwold spoke and grasped his shield (he was an old companion); he shook his ash-wood spear and exhorted the men right boldly: "Thoughts must be braver, heart more valiant, courage the greater as our strength grows less. Here lies our lord, all cut down, the hero in the dust. Long may he mourn who thinks now to turn from the battle-play. I am old in years; I will not leave the field, but think to lie by my lord's side, by the man I held so dear."

So too Godric, AEthelgar's son, emboldened them all to battle. Often he launched his javelin, his deadly spear, upon the Vikings; thus he advanced in the forefront of the host; he hewed and laid low, until he too fell in the strife. It was not the same Godric that fled from the battle.

NOTES TO CHAPTER I

1. *The Middle Ages,* rev. ed. (New York: Henry Holt, 1958), p. 169.
2. From one of the earliest extant Anglo-Saxon poems, "The Wanderer," from *Old English Poetry,* ed. and trans. John Duncan Spaeth (Princeton, N.J.: Princeton University Press, 1921), p. 140. Reprinted by permission of the publisher.
3. Dorothy Whitelock, *The Beginning of English Society* (Harmondsworth, Middlesex: Penguin Books, 1952), p. 45.
4. C. L. Wrenn, "The Poetry of Caedmon," *Proceedings of the British Academy* 32 (London, 1946): 286.
5. Grant McColley, *Paradise Lost: An Account of Its Growth and Major Origins* (Chicago: Packard & Co., 1940), pp. 21-42.
6. F. M. Stenton, *Anglo-Saxon England* (Oxford, 1943), p. 371.
7. R. H. Hodgkin, *A History of the Anglo-Saxons,* 3rd ed., 2 vols. (London: Oxford University Press, 1952), 1:202-3.
8. C. Warren Hollister, *Anglo-Saxon Military Institutions* (Oxford: Clarendon Press, 1962), pp. 10-11, 63-115. A hide of land was about 100-120 acres.
9. D. P. Kirby, *The Making of Early England* (New York: Schocken Books, 1968), pp. 120-21.

CHAPTER II

Medieval Monastic Life

ONE RESPONSE TO the contradiction between Christian ideals and the chaotic, warlike society which prevailed after the fall of Rome was to withdraw from the world—to dedicate oneself to a life of prayer and ascetic self-denial. The extreme form of such withdrawal can be found in the medieval anchorite or hermit. In the West, as opposed to the eastern Mediterranean, the hermitic way of life remained rare but those who chose it won popular respect. An English example is Saint Godric (early 12th century). According to tradition he was a poor Saxon who became a successful merchant. Turning from his wealth he finally determined to become a hermit. For years he dwelt in a cave near Durham, living in the following manner:

> He burnt boughs and branches of trees to ashes, which he mixed with his barley flour in such proportion that the ashes formed one third of the whole; and he restrained the passions of the body by weeping, watching, and fasting, so that sometimes he passed six days without eating. . . . To quench the burnings of the flesh, he subdued his body by the use of the harshest sackcloth, and for fifty years wore a coat of mail. His table was a broad flat stone, on which stood his bread, such as I have described it, but he never tasted it until compelled by absolute necessity: his drink was a moderate draught of water, and only when urged by extreme thirst; he never reposed in a bed, but would lie on the ground when he was fatigued, with his sackcloth under him, and with his head reclining on the stone which served him for a table. When the moon shone, he devoted himself to his works, and, shaking off sleep,

spent his time in prayer. In winter amid snow and hail, he entered the river naked, and there, during the whole night, offered himself up a living victim to the Lord, immersed up to his neck, and in this state poured forth psalms, and prayers, and tears.[1]

A less extreme and far more important response to the evils of the world found expression in the communal monastic movement. In the Celtic church, monks, such as those at Iona and Lindisfarne, lived in a community but retained considerable independence. The effective organization of Western monasticism appeared with the founding of the Benedictine Order in Italy in the 6th century. When Saint Augustine landed in Kent in 597, he not only renewed Britain's ties with Roman Christianity, he also introduced the Benedictine Rule. The first archbishop of Canterbury had been prior of a monastery in Rome before Pope Gregory sent him on his mission to the Anglo-Saxons.

Under the Benedictine Rule the monk lived under strict discipline, taking vows of poverty and chastity. In the words of Ailred, abbot of Rievaulx: "If we would be perfect, our Savior tells us, we must sell all that we have and give it to the poor, so that we may hereafter follow him. There are some, he says, who make themselves eunuchs for the kingdom of heaven. . . . To lead a life of complete chastity, to give up the world, to take on a more austere life—these sacrifices are freely made." [2]

The early monastic movements, as well as each new wave of reform (Cluniac, Cistercian, Dominican, and Franciscan), represented attempts to create a kind of spiritual elite who would surrender their lives to a literal following of the gospels.

Unlike the hermit, the monk worked as well as prayed, and monasteries engaged in a diversity of activities—farming, education, the care of the sick, among others.

As they acquired land and property they became increasingly involved in secular life. In time the leaders of the regular clergy (abbots and priors) found themselves, like the bishops, enmeshed in the feudal system as landlords and vassals.

It is difficult to overstate the importance of monasticism to medieval religion and civilization. On the other hand, the specific contributions of monasticism have sometimes been exaggerated. Scholars, such as G. G. Coulton, suggest that in particular the monks early neglected Saint Benedict's admonition in favor of manual labor, that actually few engaged in copying manuscripts or teaching, that charitable activities of religious houses were modest. Still, Coulton readily admits that "there was no age in which the standard of cloistered practice was not on the whole higher than that of the average layman outside; and, in certain times and places, the monks were the very salt of the earth." [3]

Saint Anselm as Monk and Archbishop (ca. 1110)

Saint Anselm was one of the most distinguished medieval churchmen. He became a famous scholar, and as archbishop of Canterbury served as primate of England from 1093 to 1109. Born in Italy, Anselm moved to France, where he entered orders. He rose to become abbot of Bec, probably the most influential Norman monastery. In 1079 Anselm made a tour of Bec's daughter houses in England and thereafter became well known to English churchmen. During another English visit in 1093, King William II named him archbishop of Canterbury. From then until his death in 1109 Anselm was closely involved in English affairs. His biography enlightens several aspects of English medieval life: the nature of the monastic ideal, the close ties between England and Normandy, the international character of the medieval church, and the troubled relations between church and state.

Eadmer, his biographer, was a monk of Christ Church Cathedral, Canterbury, who first met Anselm in 1079. Later, after Anselm was appointed archbishop, Eadmer became his constant companion. He soon began taking notes in preparation for writing a biography of Anselm. Although the archbishop ordered him to abandon the project, he secretly kept a copy of his manuscript and completed it after Anselm's death. Since Eadmer viewed Anselm as a saint, the biography idealizes its subject, but for that very reason it provides a vivid picture of the perfect monk striving amid the temptations and distractions of a sinful world to dedicate his life to God's service.

The first part of the following selections is from Eadmer's biography and tells of Anselm's early career and of his difficult relations with William Rufus. The second part is from another work by Eadmer, called *The History of Recent Events in England*. This gives an account of the Compromise of Bec, which resolved the struggle between Anselm and King Henry I over lay investiture. As Norman Cantor expresses it: "Lay investiture was still a very meaningful institution. While the retention of ecclesiastical homage would allow the king to retain his power over the English Church, the surrender of lay investiture meant the virtual abandonment of the idea of theocratic monarchy in England. This surrender of the intellectual basis of royal authority over the church Henry was in no hurry to make." [4] The concession that Pope Paschal and Anselm made permitted the king to require homage from ecclesiastics for the fiefs they held; in return, Henry agreed to recognize the sole right of the church to invest abbots and bishops into their spiritual offices.

The Life of Saint Anselm
BOOK I

iv. *How he left his native land because of his father's great hostility to him.*

From that time, with health of body, youth and worldly well-being smiling upon him, he began little by little to cool in the fervour of his desire for a religious life—so much so that he began to desire to go the way of the world rather than to leave the world for a monastic life. He gradually turned from study, which had formerly been his chief occupation, and began to give himself up to youthful amusements. His love and reverence for his mother held him back to some extent from these paths, but she died and then the ship of his heart had, as it were, lost its anchor and drifted almost entirely among the waves of the world. But Almighty God, foreseeing what he was going to make of him, stirred up for him a hateful and domestic strife, lest in enjoying a transitory peace he should lose his soul. That is to say, he stirred up in his father's mind so keen a hatred against him that he persecuted him as much, or even more, for the things he did well as for those which he did ill. Nor could he soften his father by any degree of humility, but the more humble he showed himself towards his father, the sharper did he feel his father's anger toward him. When he saw that this was becoming more than he could bear, he feared that worse might come of it, and he chose rather to renounce both his patrimony and his country than to bring some disgrace upon either himself or his father by continuing to live with him. He gathered together those things which were necessary for the journey, and left his country, with a clerk as his companion and servant. . . .

v. *How he went to Lanfranc, a man of great prudence, and became his pupil; and how he deliberated where to become a monk.*

After passing almost three years from this time, partly in Burgundy and partly in France, he went to Normandy to see, to talk to, and stay with a certain master by the name of Lanfranc, a truly good man and one of real nobility in the excellence of his religious life and wisdom. His lofty fame had resounded everywhere and had drawn to him the best clerks from all parts of the world. Anselm therefore came to him and recognised the outstanding wisdom, which shone forth in him. He placed himself under his guidance and in a short time became the most intimate of his disciples. He gave himself up day and night to literary studies, not only reading with Lanfranc those things which he wished, but teaching carefully to others the things which they required. While he was thus wearying his body with late nights, with cold and with hunger because of his studies, he began to think that if he had become a monk somewhere, as he formerly intended, he would not have had to put up with anything more severe than what he was now suffering, nor would he then lose the reward of his labour, which he was quite uncertain of retaining in his present state. When this had once entered his head, he began to turn his whole intention to pleasing God; and, despising the world and its pleasures, he desired in very truth to become a monk. And what then? He turned over in his mind where he could best bring to pass what he desired, and he argued thus with himself: "Well then, I shall become a monk. But where? If at Cluny or at Bec, all the time I have spent in study will be lost. For at Cluny the severity of the order, and at Bec the outstanding ability of Lanfranc, who is a monk there, will condemn me either to fruitlessness or insignificance. Let me therefore carry out my plan somewhere where I can both display my knowledge and be of service to others." He often used playfully to recount these thoughts of his, and he would add: "I was not yet tamed, and there was not yet in me any strong contempt of the world. Hence when I said this, as I thought, out of love for others, I did not see how damnable it was." But after a while he came to himself. "What?" he said. "Is this being a monk—to desire to be set over others, to receive more honour and glory than others? Far from it. So put aside your rebelliousness and become a monk in that place where, rightly and for God's sake, you will be lowest of all, and where you will be most insignificant and be held in less esteem than all others. And where can this be? At Bec, of course. For there I shall be of no weight, so long as he is there who is conspicuous by the light of his pre-eminent wisdom, who is adequate to all calls, and who is honoured and acceptable to all. There I shall have rest, there God will be to me all in all, there His love will be the only subject of my contemplation, the blessed and unremitting memory of Him will there be my sweet solace and satisfaction." . . .

vi. *How he became a monk on the advice of Lanfranc and Maurilius, archbishop of Rouen.*

Sometimes also at that time he was attracted by other walks in life, but on this chiefly were his desires fixed. Knowing therefore that it is written, "Do all things with counsel, and when they are done you will not repent," he was unwilling to commit himself unadvisedly to any one of the walks of life on which his thoughts were turned, lest he should seem in anything to disobey the commands of Holy Scripture. He had many friends besides Lanfranc, but when he came to choose that one counsellor in a thousand on whom he could rely utterly in these matters, he chose Lanfranc. He came to him and told him that he was undecided between three courses of action, but that he would hold to the one which Lanfranc judged best and reject the other two. He expounded to him the three aims, as follows: "I want," he said, "either to be a monk, or to dwell in a hermitage, or to live on my family estate, ministering so far as I can to the poor, in God's name, if you advise it"—for his father had died by this time and all the inheritance had come to him. "Know then, my lord Lanfranc, that these are the three things between which my will fluctuates; but I beg that you will stablish me in the one which you think best." Lanfranc hesitated to give an opinion and advised that the matter should be taken to be heard by the venerable Maurilius, archbishop of Rouen. Anselm acquiesced in this plan, and together with Lanfranc he went to the archbishop. . . . They came then to the bishop, explained the reason for their coming, and asked him what he thought about it. Without hesitation the monastic life was extolled beyond the others, and the monastic profession recommended before all others. Anselm heard and approved. Then, setting aside all else, he left the world and became a monk at Bec, being then in his twenty-seventh year.

vii. *How he was made prior, and how one night while engaged in holy meditation he saw through a wall with his physical sight the things which were taking place on the other side of it.*

The monastery was ruled at this time by an abbot, Dom Herlwin by name, a man of great age and well known for his upright life. It was he who had built the monastery from its foundations on his own patrimony, and he was its first abbot. Lanfranc, whom we have often mentioned already, held the office of prior. And now Anselm, being a new monk, set himself to imitate the lives of the more religious among the monks. Indeed he so performed every religious duty, that if anyone in the whole community wished to lead a religious life, he had in Anselm a pattern which he could follow. So, for three years, he grew daily in stature, and was held in honour and esteem. Then when Lanfranc was taken away to govern the monastery at Caen, Anselm succeeded to the office of prior. Having thus obtained a larger liberty for the service of God, he began to devote his whole self and his whole time to serving God, and he put the world and all its affairs entirely behind him. And so it came about that, being continually given up to God and to spiritual exercises, he attained such a height of divine speculation, that he was able by God's help to see into and unravel many most obscure and previously insoluble questions about the divinity of God and about our faith, and to prove by plain arguments that what he said was firm and catholic truth. For he had so much faith in the Holy Scriptures, that he firmly and inviolably believed that there was nothing in them which deviated in any way from the path of solid truth. Hence he applied his whole mind to this end, that according to his faith he might be found worthy to see with the eye of reason those things in the Holy Scriptures which, as he felt, lay hidden in a deep obscurity. Thus one night it happened that he was lying awake on his bed before matins exercised in mind about these matters; and as he meditated he tried to puzzle out how the prophets of old could see both past and future as if they were present and set them forth beyond doubt in speech or writing. And, behold, while he was thus absorbed in striving with all his might to understand this problem, he fixed his eyes on the wall—right through the masonry of the church and dormitory—he saw the monks whose office it was to prepare for matins going about the altar and other parts of the church lighting the candles; and finally he saw one of them take in his hands the bell-rope and sound the bell to awaken the brethren. At this sound the whole community rose from their beds, and Anselm was astonished at the thing which had happened. From this he saw that it was a very small thing for God to show to the prophets in the spirit the things which would come to pass, since God had allowed him to see with his bodily eyes through so many obstacles the things which then were happening.

ix. *How he converted the hatred which some felt for him into genuine love.*

At first then after he became prior some of the brethren of the monastery were his enemies, being envious at seeing him, whom in seniority of profession they judged ought to have come after them, preferred before them. Being thus upset, they upset others; they spread scandal, they made dissensions, they formed cliques and fostered hatreds. But to those who hated peace, he showed himself peaceful. He repaid their detractions with the offices of brotherly charity, preferring to overcome evil with good rather than, in wrong-doing, to be overcome by their wickedness. In this purpose, by God's mercy, he succeeded, inasmuch that they—perceiving that he walked purely and innocently in all his ways and that there was nothing in him for which he could rightly be reproached—changed their evil intention to a good one, and began in well-doing to emulate his words and deeds. In order to make it clear how this happened, I shall take one of them as an example; and by seeing how he was turned from his evil ways by Anselm's guile, we may gather how others also were corrected by him.

xxii. *Concerning the discretion which he taught a certain abbot to practise towards boys who were being educated in his school.*

On one occasion then, a certain abbot, who was considered to be a sufficiently religious man, was talking with him about matters of monastic discipline, and among other things he said something about the boys brought up in the cloister, adding: "What, I ask you, is to be done with them? They are incorrigible ruffians. We never give over beating them day and night, and they only get worse and worse." Anselm replied with astonishment: "You never give over beating them? And what are they like when they grow up?" "Stupid brutes," he said. To which Anselm retorted, "You have spent your energies in rearing them to good purpose: from men you have reared beasts." "But what can we do about it?" he said; "We use every means to force them to get better, but without success." "You force them? Now tell me, my lord abbot, if you plant a tree-shoot in your garden, and straightway shut it in on every side so that it has no space to put out its branches, what kind of a tree will you have in after years when you let it out of its confinement?" "A useless one, certainly, with its branches all twisted and knotted." "And whose fault would this be, except your own for shutting it in so unnaturally? Without doubt, this is what you do with your boys. At their oblation they are planted in the garden of the Church, to grow and bring forth fruit for God. But you so terrify them and hem them in on all sides with threats and blows that they are utterly deprived of their liberty. And being thus injudiciously oppressed, they harbour and welcome and nurse within themselves evil and crooked thoughts like thorns, and cherish these thoughts so passionately that they doggedly reject everything which could minister to their correction. Hence, feeling no love or pity, good-will or tenderness in your attitude towards them, they have in future no faith in your goodness but believe that all your actions proceed from hatred and malice against them. The deplorable result is that as they grow in body so their hatred increases, together with their apprehension of evil, and are forward in all crookedness and vice. They have been brought up in no true charity towards anyone, so they regard everyone with suspicion and jealousy. But, in God's name, I would have you tell me why you are so incensed against them. Are they not human? Are they not flesh and blood like you? Would you like to have been treated as you treat them, and to have become what they now are? Now consider this. You wish to form them in good habits by blows and chastisement alone. Have you ever seen a goldsmith form his leaves of gold or silver into a beautiful figure with blows alone? I think not. How then does he work? In order to mould his leaf into a suitable form he now presses it and strikes it gently with his tool, and now even more gently raises it with careful pressure and gives it shape. So, if you want your boys to be adorned with good habits, you too, besides the pressure of blows, must apply the encouragement and help of fatherly sympathy and gentleness." To which the abbot replied: "What encouragement? What help? We do all we can to force them into sober and manly habits." "Good," said Anselm, "just as bread and all kinds of solid food are good and wholesome for those who can digest them; but feed a suckling infant on such food, take away its milk, and you will see him strangled rather than strengthened by his diet. The reason for this is too obvious to need explanation, but this is the lesson to remember: just as weak and strong bodies have each their own food appropriate to their condition, so weak and strong souls need to be fed according to their capacity. The strong soul delights in and is refreshed by solid food, such as patience in tribulation, not coveting one's neighbour's goods, offering the other cheek, praying for one's enemies, loving those who hate us, and many similar things. But the weak soul, which is still inexperienced in the service of God, needs milk—gentleness from others, kindness, compassion, cheerful encouragement, loving forbearance, and much else of the same kind. If you adapt yourself in this way according to the strength and weakness of those under you, you will by the grace of God win them all for God, so far at least as your efforts can." When the abbot heard this, he was sorrowful, and said, "We have indeed wandered from the way of truth, and the light of discretion has not lighted our way." And he fell on the ground at Anselm's feet confessing himself as a miserable sinner, seeking pardon for the past, and promising amendment in the future.

BOOK II

i. *How Anselm came to England and was received by King William the younger.*

When the renowned William king of the English died, his son William inherited his kingdom. Then the venerable father Lanfranc departed this life, and William oppressed the churches and monasteries throughout England most harshly. In the fourth year of this oppression Anselm was invited, nay urgently entreated and required, to come to England by Hugh earl of Chester and many other noblemen of the English kingdom, who had chosen him as their spiritual physician and protector; and being moreover constrained by the prayer and command laid upon him by his own church for their common good, he came to England. Thus on the eve of the Nativity of the Blessed and ever Virgin Mother of God, he arrived at Canterbury. Here many of the monks and laity, as if foretelling the future, acclaimed him as archbishop; wherefore he left the place early next morning and on no account would consent to celebrate the Feast there, as they besought him to do. Moreover when he came to the royal court all the nobility eagerly met him and received him with great honour. The king himself rose from his throne, and met him at the door of his hall with joy; he fell on his neck and led him by the hand to his seat. They sat down, and for a while exchanged cheerful conversation. Then Anselm asked the others to go apart so that he could talk privately with the king. He put aside the business of the monastery, which was supposed to be his chief reason for coming there, and began to rebuke the king for those things which were reported about him: nor did he pass over in silence anything which he knew ought to be said to him. For almost everyone in the whole kingdom daily talked about him, in private and in public, saying such things as by no means befitted the dignity of a king. When they had finished talking they parted, and Anselm said nothing on that occasion about the business of his church. Then he went off to the earl of Chester and was obliged to remain a considerable time in those parts.

ii. *How the king fell ill and chose Anselm as archbishop; and how Anselm refused to consent despite the use of force.*

Meanwhile King William was stricken with a serious illness and came to the point of death. His barons persuaded him, among other things, to take thought for the mother of his whole kingdom, namely the church of Canterbury, and to relieve her long widowhood and misfortune by the appointment of an archbishop. He acquiesced in this advice, and declared that Anselm was the man most fitted for this work. There was universal acclamation, and both clergy and people commended the king's judgment without a single voice being raised in contradiction. When Anselm heard this, he wore himself almost to death in his objections, and in resisting and fighting against it. But united body of the Church of God prevailed. So he was seized, and forcibly carried rather than led into the neighbouring church with hymns and rejoicings. This took place in the year of our Lord's Incarnation 1093, on 6 March, being the first Sunday in Lent.

v. *How and why the king's mind was turned against him.*

Afterwards he presented himself at the royal court at Christmas time, and was honourably received by the king. He passed the first three days of the Feast pleasantly with the king. But then the king's mind was turned against him, at the instigation of the devil and of evil men, because he refused to despoil his tenants in order to give the king £1,000 as a thank-offering for his munificence. So, having angered his lord, he left the court.

viii. *His great grief at the loss of his former tranquility of mind.*

When Anselm began now to think of all the peace he had lost and all the labour he had found, his spirit was torn and tormented with bitter anguish. For he saw in his mind's eye the life which he had been accustomed to lead as prior and as abbot—how joyfully he had reposed and delighted in the love of God and of his neighbour, how devoutly he had been heard by all to whom he ministered the words of life, how still more devoutly his hearers had hastened to put into practice what he taught, and thereby (as he hoped) added to the sum of his reward. And now how different it was! As a bishop he ought to have gone on to better things; but he saw his days and nights taken up with secular business; he saw himself unable to devote his attention either to God or to his neighbour in God's name as he formerly had done; and he saw no-one willing to listen to the Word of life from his lips or to carry it out; and thereby he lost (as he thought) his reward. To add to these evils of his own, the cruel oppression of his men daily afflicted his ears; and he was deafened by the threats of worse to follow, made by malicious men on all sides. For it was well known that the king's mind was worked up into a fury against him, and as a result every wicked man thought himself happy if he could hit on any device to exasperate him further. . . .

Selections on Anselm from Eadmer's
Recent Events in England

Now at this time it was the fashion for nearly all the young men of the Court to grow their hair long like girls; then, with locks well combed, glancing about them and winking in ungodly fashion, they would daily walk abroad with delicate steps and mincing gait. Accordingly Father Anselm made these things the subject of his sermon delivered at the beginning of Lent in the presence of the people who flocked to his mass and to the sprinkling of the ashes. By so doing he brought a great number of them to repentance with the result that they cut their hair short and adopted again such bearing as becomes a man. Those whom he could not recall from this degradation he suspended from reception of the ashes and from the blessing of his absolution.

In all such cases, as in the incident just mentioned, it was Anselm's way to act freely but at the same time discreetly, keeping ever before his eyes regard for nothing but what was just and right. In this spirit he set himself most earnestly to see how he could provoke the King to the service of God and the maintenance of justice. Accordingly he came one day to the King, as he often did, and sitting down beside him began a conversation by saying, "You have, my Lord King, determined to cross the sea and to subdue Normandy. That these and other projects upon which you have set your heart may turn out prosperously, as you would wish, I beg you first of all to give help and guidance to secure that in this Kingdom of yours Christianity, which among the majority of the inhabitants has almost entirely died out, may be restored to its rightful place." The King replied, "What help? What guidance?" Anselm answered: "Command, if you will, that Councils such as were held in the old days be revived, that wrongs committed be brought to light, when brought to light be examined, when examined be censured and so censured be checked. No general Council of Bishops has in fact been held in England since you became King, nor for several years before that. In consequence of this there has been a widespread of crimes, which for want of anyone to prune them back have through evil usage grown to all too exuberant strength." The King said, "I will deal with these things when I think fit, not at your pleasure but at mine. I will consider all that at some other time." And he added mockingly, "But you, what would you speak about in such a Council?" To this Anselm replied: "That most shameful crime of sodomy, not to speak of illicit marriages between persons of kindred blood and other wicked dealings in things abominable, that crime, I say, of sodomy, but lately spread abroad in this land, has already borne fruit all too abundantly and has with its abomination defiled many. If it be not speedily met with sentence of stern judgment coming from you and by rigorous discipline on the part of the Church, the whole land will, I declare, become little better than Sodom itself. I beseech you, let us two make a united effort, you with your power as King, I with my authority as archbishop, to establish some decree against it such that, when it is published up and down the land, even the hearing of it will make everyone that is addicted to such practices tremble and be dismayed." These things found no home in the heart of the King and he made but brief answer saying, "What good would that do for you?" "If not for me," said Anselm, "it should, I trust, do so for God and for you." "Enough," said the King, "say no more about it." So Anselm fell silent; but presently addressed himself to other matters and said: "There is another matter to which I would have you give serious consideration and doing so extend a helping hand as on such consideration shall seem expedient. There are in this land very many Abbeys bereft of their pastors. In consequence of this the monks, forsaking the rule of their order, give themselves up to the luxuries of the world and then pass from this life unconfessed. I advise you, beseech you, warn you, to look diligently into this, which is a matter of the gravest importance, and to appoint to these Abbeys according to the will of God, lest in destroying the monasteries and ruining the monks you bring damnation (which God forbid) upon yourself." Then the King could no longer restrain himself and greatly roused said angrily, "What business is that of yours? Are not the Abbeys mine? You do as you like with your manors and shall not I do as I like with my Abbeys?" Anselm replied, "They are yours to defend and guard as their patron; but not yours to assault or to lay waste. We know that they are God's to provide a living for his ministers, not to provide the means for carrying on your campaigns and wars. You have surely manors and revenues enough from which you can plentifully supply your needs. Leave, if you please, to the Churches what is theirs." "You can be quite sure," said the King, "that all that you are saying is utterly repugnant to me. Your predecessor would never have dared to say such things to my father; and I will do nothing for you." Then Anselm realized that he was casting his words to the wind, so he rose up and departed. . . .

Meanwhile a rumour spread through the various countries that Urban, the Pope, had ended his life in this world. In fact he died before he received the reply on Anselm's case which he was expecting from the King of England. When his death came to the ears of that King he exclaimed, "The hatred of God rest upon whoever cares a rap for that!" He then went on to ask, "But the new Pope, what sort of man is he?" When told that in some respects he was like Archbishop Anselm, he said: "By the face of God, if he is like that, he is no good. But let him keep strictly to himself, for his popedom shall not get the upper hand of me this time; to that I take my oath; meantime I have gained my freedom and shall do freely as I like." He had the idea that not even the Pope of the whole world could have any jurisdiction in his realm unless it were by his permission. But how he behaved after this is not in place to write of here, as I must hasten on to deal with other matters. But he was not long allowed to enjoy the liberty which he boasted he had gained. Less than a year elapsed before he lost it altogether, being himself struck down by an unexpected and sudden death. October [1099] heard him so boasting; the second day of the following August saw him dying. On that day after having breakfasted he went out into the forest to hunt and there, struck by an arrow that pierced his heart, impenitent and unconfessed, he died instantly and was at once forsaken by everyone. Whether, as some say, that arrow struck him in its flight or, as the majority declare, he stumbled and falling violently upon it met his death, is a question we think unnecessary to go into; sufficient to know that by the just judgment of God he was stricken down and slain.

In this connection there comes to mind what that King once said, as we have recorded above, to the Bishop of Rochester; that God would never find him become good in return for the evil which God had done to him. I reflect too how afterwards God dealt with him so long as he lived. It is common knowledge that from the time he uttered those words, after he had recovered from the sickness by which, as is well known, he had been laid low, he had such success in overcoming and conquering his enemies, in acquiring territories, in giving free play to his desires, that you would suppose that all the world was smiling upon him. . . . In short, he was, I declare, so prospered in all his doings that it was as if God was saying in answer to his words, "If, as you say, I shall never find you become good in return for evil, I will try whether instead I can find you become good in return for good, and so in all that you consider good I will fulfil your wishes." But what was the result? Why, he proceeded step by step so far in his evil ways that, as those who by day and by night were present and saw his actions bear witness, he never got up in the morning or went to bed at night without being every time a worse man than when he last went to bed or last got up. So, since he refused either to be disciplined by ill fortune or to be led to right-doing by good fortune, to prevent his raging with fury long continued to the detriment of all good men, the just Judge by a death sharp and swift cut short his life in this world. . . .

What oppression in many forms the whole of England suffered during this time and how severe that oppression was, it is I know difficult to describe. The King [Henry I], because he had not succeeded in subduing the whole of Normandy in the way we have described, leaving that country returned to England in order that, armed with a more plentiful supply of money, he could return and conquer the remainder, thereby ousting his brother from his inheritance. In the collection of this money the collectors shewed no regard for piety or pity; but, as persons coming from England assured us, extortion, frightful and cruel, beat down like a raging storm upon all. Then you might see, so they reported, those who in fact had nothing to give driven out from their cottages or the doors of their houses torn away and carried off and themselves left open to be plundered of everything; or their paltry bits of furniture would be taken and they reduced to abject poverty, or at any rate ground down and tormented with some form of wretchedness or another. But against those who seemed to have everything, certain new and carefully thought out forms of confiscation were applied and in this way, as they dared not institute a suit in their own defence against the King of the country, their possessions were taken and they themselves plunged into serious hardship. These proceedings will perhaps be considered by some to be hardly worth mentioning considering that it was not only in King Henry's time that they were adopted but that many like them were practised in the time of his brother, to say nothing of King William, their father. But these exactions seemed heavier and more intolerable than the earlier because generally much less was found which could be taken from subjects who had been already stripped and beggared. And there is this further to be said; in the Council of London, as we have said above, all priests and canons in England were prohibited from association with women and this prohibition had during Anselm's absence in exile been disobeyed by very many of them, who had never parted from their women or, if they had, had taken them back again. Accordingly the King, not willing to let this sin go unpunished, instructed his agents to institute proceedings against them and to take their money by way of expiation of this sin. But, when very many of them were found innocent of this offence, the money, which was in fact being sought for the Prince's needs, did not yield so large an amount as the collectors had had reason to expect. So the ruling was altered or rather was turned right round so as to include the innocent with the guilty, and all churches which had parishes were put under contribution and each having a certain sum of money charged upon it was ordered to effect its redemption by payment made through the person who served God in that Church. So everywhere was a spectacle of misery. . . .

It should, however, be mentioned that such were the evils that swept like a flood over England in those days that the very bishops who, as can be gathered from what was said above, siding with the Prince had tried continually to restrict the liberty of the Church and Anselm himself when he sought to uphold and guard that liberty, now, constrained by the enormity of such evils, despatched a letter with a message to Anselm, humbly asking for his help and support, and promising that from now on they would in all matters divine follow him as Father. . . .

Meanwhile, as messengers were frequently coming from England to Normandy, the policy which the King was putting into execution in the treatment of the priests in England was published far and wide, and not only those who gloated over all that was to the King's discredit but even those who fed upon his praise were led to hate and denounce him. Anselm, unable to bear such evil-speaking of the King and anxious to reclaim him from such wrongdoing, wrote to him. . . .

> To Henry, his most dear lord, by the grace of God King of England, Anselm, Archibishop of Canterbury, sends his faithful prayers and faithful service.
> It is my duty, if I hear that you are doing anything which is not to the good of your soul, not to fail to tell you of it, lest, which God forbid, He be angry both with you for doing what is not pleasing to Him and with me for keeping silence. Now I hear that your Excellency is inflicting punishment upon the priests in England and exacting fines from them for not having kept the injunction of the Council which I, with other bishops and persons professed

in religion, with your gracious approval held in London. This is a proceeding which up to now has been unheard of and unprecedented in the Church of God on the part of any King or any prince. By the law of God it is not for anyone except the bishops, each in his own diocese, to punish an offence of that sort or, if the bishops are themselves negligent in this, then for the Archbishop and Primate. Therefore, as my most dear lord, for whose soul I care more than for my own life, I beg you and in true loyalty to your person body and soul alike I urge you not to act contrary to the custom of the Church by intermeddling with so grave a sin; and, if you have already begun so acting, to give up doing so altogether. I must tell you that you have good reason to fear, for any money so taken, not to mention all the harm it does to your soul, however much it may promote your earthly projects at the time it is spent, will prove all the more disastrous to them in the end. Finally, you know that in Normandy you restored to me your goodwill and repossessed me of my archbishopric. Watching for and punishing such an offence is a part, and a most important part, of the duty attaching to the archbishopric, seeing that I am a bishop much more for exercising spiritual charge than for holding earthly property.

May almighty God so direct your heart in this and all your doings according to His will that after this life He may bring you to His glory. Amen.

The Pope sent the following letter to Anselm:

> Paschal, Bishop, servant of the servants of God, to his venerable brother Anselm, Archbishop of Canterbury, greeting and apostolic blessing.
>
> That almighty God most high has inclined the heart of the King of England to obey the Apostolic See, for this we give thanks to that same Lord of mercies in whose hand the hearts of kings are held. We feel no doubt at all that it is due to your gracious charity and to your persistent prayers that this has been brought about, that in this respect God on high should look mercifully upon that people over whom you with such anxious care preside.
>
> You must understand that, in making such concession as we are making to the King and to those who seem to deserve punishment, we do this from motives of affection and sympathy to enable us to raise up those that are fallen. Whoever, while himself standing, offers his hand to one that is fallen to raise him up, cannot succeed

in doing so without himself stooping. Although by so bending he seems to come very near falling, yet stooping does not involve losing his own balance. So we now absolve you, our venerable and most dear brother, in Christ, from that prohibition, or as you believe it to have been, excommunication which you know was pronounced by our predecessor, Pope Urban of sacred memory, against investitures and acts of homage. Accordingly, those who have accepted investiture or have consecrated those so invested or have done homage do you with the help of the Lord receive back into fellowship on their making the amends which we have instructed William and Baldwin, the envoys of the King and yourself respectively, loyal and truthful men, to make known to you. On our authority absolve them; and then either consecrate them yourself or instruct whoever you choose to do so, unless, as may be the case, you find that they are guilty of some other offence for which they ought to be debarred from the higher offices of the Church. . . .

In future, apart from investitures of churches, any who take preferments, even if they have done homage to the King, are by no means to be banned on that account from the rite of consecration until by the grace of almighty God the heart of the King is softened by your preaching, like ground refreshed by the rains, to the extent of giving up this practice altogether.

Then again as to the bishops who, as you know, took back from us a false report, against them our heart is greatly hardened because they have not only wronged us but have deceived the souls of many simple folk and have driven the King into opposition to the loving care of the Apostolic See. With the help of the Lord we shall not allow their crime to go unpunished. Nevertheless, since our son, the King, besets us with persistent and urgent intercession on their behalf, even to them you are not to refuse the right to share in your fellowship until they receive a summons to appear before us.

The King and his consort and those chiefs who on our instruction have exerted themselves in the King's court over this business and will endeavour yet further to do so, whose names the said William will privately make known to you, you must absolve from their penances and sins, as we have promised should be done.

Since the Lord almighty has granted us in the Kingdom of England to progress thus far in this policy of reform to His glory and that of His Church, do you, my Brother, now bring to bear upon the King and princes such gentleness, tact, wisdom and foresight that those things which have not yet been set right as they should be may with the help of our Lord God through your devoted care be duly amended. You can be sure that in this task you, who love us, have our full support, so that what you loose we loose, what you bind we bind too. . . .

Dated the 23rd March. [1106]

When William arrived in England and reported to the King what progress had been made over his business with the Pope,[5] the King, greatly pleased at what he heard, at once sent him back with a message to Anselm asking him to return to his Church. Accordingly only a few days later William returned to us; but he then found Anselm laid up. At this he was greatly disconcerted. For he was now already wholeheartedly set on the liberation of the Church and was exerting himself anxiously to do all he possibly could to secure that Anselm should be restored to his See in peace and honour. So, afraid that Anselm might be hindered from moving to England quite as much by his affection for Bec and the brethren there as by the illness from which he was suffering, he proceeded to exert all possible influence both personally and through us, who were with Anselm, to tear him away from Bec and start him upon the journey he was so anxious he should take. Accordingly, beginning with messages of entreaty imploring him as from his lord, the King of England, to hasten his return and come to England, which was disconsolate at his absence, he declared, and not only declared but promised, that the King himself was fully determined to meet Anselm's wishes in whatever he should thenceforth direct, and that most readily, and was anxious no longer to have any disagreement with the Church of Rome. He ended by saying, "Let nothing whatever, I implore you, delay your coming lest by evil chance some gust of worldly interest break out to turn the King away from these good intentions." Hearing this Anselm thanked God for his wonderful gift and, after obtaining leave of the brethren with whom we had now lived, greatly loved and greatly honoured, for such a long time, he came to Jumieges on his way to England. But there a fresh attack of the illness which, as we have recorded, had overtaken him at Bec made it impossible for him to proceed any further. So he sent messengers to England to let the King know what it was that was delaying his return. At this report the King was troubled and greatly grieved, swearing by the word of God that no loss would trouble him so much as would Anselm's death. Accordingly he sent back messengers as quickly as possible begging the Archbishop to take care of himself and to take every opportunity of resting. He also told him to take as he liked of all that was at the King's disposal in Normandy and to order of it as much as was needed to be supplied to himself and his companions. He added that he was to expect the King to come over to Normandy in the following month. Anselm received this message gratefully and remained at Jumieges about a month. Then being considerably recovered from his illness he returned to Bec, thinking that it would be more convenient and more proper to await the King's coming there than anywhere else. But just when all were rejoicing enthusiastically at his return, suddenly a lamentable misfortune occurred to upset their happiness. Anselm was again taken so seriously ill that we did not expect anything but his death. The Bishops and Abbots of Normandy came flocking to Bec and were all discussing arrangements for his funeral when, contrary to all expectations, almighty God of His goodness restored him to health and thereby brought great joy to many.

Then on the day of the Assumption of the Blessed Mary [15 August 1106] the King came to Bec and, after a solemn mass had been celebrated by Anselm, the King and he met and so at last all the disputes which had drawn them apart found peace and concord. The Churches of England which, as recorded much earlier in this work, King William, the brother of King Henry, had let out at rent, which had never been done before, the King now restored to Anselm's hands free of that exaction and further promised that so long as he lived he would not take anything from the Churches during any period that they were without a pastor. As for the money which he had taken from the priests, as we described above, he undertook so to put the matter right that those who had so far not given anything should not give at all and those who had given should for three years enjoy all their property in peace and quietness scot-free. Furthermore all that at his command had been taken from the Archbishopric while Anselm was in exile he promised to restore when he was back in England and gave security for his so doing.

As soon as these and other matters which the circumstances of the case required had been arranged between the King and Anselm, the latter started upon his journey to return to England, and upheld by the divine protection landed at Dover sound in body and mind with all his companions. With what enthusiasm, what delight, what expectation of good to come, his arrival in England was greeted can, I think, be to some extent imagined when the evils which, as I have briefly indicated, had become rampant there before his return are borne in mind. Not to speak of the rejoicing of men of every age and rank, I will only say briefly this of the Queen herself; that no earthly concerns, no pageantry of this world's glory could keep her from going on before to the different places to which Anselm was coming; and, as the monks and canons went out as usual to meet the Archbishop, she went on ahead and by her careful forethought saw to it that his various lodgings were richly supplied with suitable furnishings.

After this those who had been put into the Churches and monasteries to extract from them money for the King were turned out and the property of each Church within and without was entrusted to its representatives for the benefit of the whole body. Moreover the cases of the priests were dealt with in accordance with the promise which, as we have said, the King had made to Anselm, and publication of the King's order to that effect was made throughout the whole Kingdom.

Meanwhile the King subdued Normandy by force of arms. . . .

Not unnaturally it was the declared opinion of many that it was in consequence of his having made peace with Anselm that the King gained this victory.

Jocelin of Brakelond
(ca. 1200)

Most medieval monastic chroniclers give an account of ecclesiastical, political, and military developments but seldom much detail of the everyday life and business of the monastery itself. Jocelin of Brakelond does just the opposite. His chronicle presents an intimate view of monastic life, and in addition tells something of the relations of the monastery with the crown, the nobility, the peasants on the abbey lands, and the townsmen of Saint Edmundsbury.

Written about 1200, the chronicle was first published in Latin in 1840, when its colorful portrait of the abbey of Saint Edmundsbury led Thomas Carlyle to write an essay, "The Ancient Monk," in *Past and Present* (1843). To Carlyle, the monk had become almost "an extinct species of the human family," but he held that Jocelin could reconstruct for us the monastic life of the past—"a wise simplicity is in him: much natural sense: a *veracity* that goes deeper than words." [6] The central figure in Jocelin's chronicle is Abbot Samson. Although a God-fearing man, Samson does not embody saintly virtues; rather, he represents the able administrator. As monasteries became well established, the requirements of estate management and the fulfillment of feudal obligations tended to crowd out their religious purposes. "There were," observes Father Knowles, "many Samsons between the reign of John and the Dissolution; it is not easy to find an Aelred or an Anselm." [7]

Jocelin, the author of the chronicle, entered Saint Edmund's about 1173. He appears to have served as Samson's chaplain for six years and then to have been appointed cellarer. According to a contemporary treatise on monastic customs, "the cellarer ought to be wise, cautious and thrifty. Everything that belongs to the monastery, whether lands or churches, with the exception of what belongs [especially] to other officials, is to be in his charge." [8]

Jocelin of Brakelond

I have been at pains to set down the things that I have seen and heard, which came to pass in the Church of St. Edmund in our days, from the year in which the Flemings were taken prisoner outside the town, that being the year in which I assumed the religious habit, and Prior Hugh was deposed and his office given to Robert; and I have included certain evil things for a warning, and certain good as an example to others. At that time Abbot Hugh was grown old and his eyes waxed somewhat dim. Pious he was and kindly, a strict monk and good, but in the business of this world neither good nor wise. For he trusted those about him overmuch and gave them too ready credence, relying always on the wisdom of others rather than his own. Discipline and religion and all things pertaining to the Rule were zealously observed within the cloister; but outside all things were badly handled, and every man did, not what he ought, but what he would, since his lord was simple and growing old. The townships of the Abbot and all the hundreds were given out to farm; the woods were destroyed, the house of the manors threatened to fall in ruin, and day by day all things went from bad to worse. The Abbot found but one remedy and one consolation—to borrow money, that thus at least he might be able to maintain the honour of his house. No Easter nor Michaelmas came round during the eight years before his death but that one or two hundred pounds were added to his debt; the bonds were continually renewed, and the interest as it grew was turned into capital. This infirmity spread from the head to the members—from the superior to his subjects. And so it came about that each obedientiary had his own seal and bound himself in debt to Jews and Christians as he pleased. Often silken copes and flasks of gold and other ornaments of the church were placed in pawn without the knowledge of the Convent. . . .

A rumour reached Abbot Hugh that Richard, Archibishop of Canterbury, desired to come to us and hold a scrutiny in our Church, by virtue of his authority as legate; and after taking counsel the Abbot sent to Rome and obtained exemption from the power of the said legate. When our messenger returned from Rome, we had not the wherewithal to pay the sums that he had promised the Lord Pope and the cardinals, except, under the circumstances, the cross that was above the High Altar and the little image of the Virgin and that of St. John, which images Stigand the Archibishop had adorned with a great weight of gold and silver, and had given to St. Edmund. Some of our brethren who were close friends of the Abbot went so far as to say that even the feretory of St. Edmund ought to be stripped of its plating to pay for such a liberty as this, not noting the great peril that might arise from such a liberty. For if there should arise some Abbot of ours who desired to dilapidate the property of our Church and to treat his Convent ill, there will be no man to whom the Convent will be able to complain of the wrongs done by the Abbot who will fear neither Bishop or Archibishop or Legate, and his impunity will make him all the bolder to do wrong. . . .

In the twenty-third year of his abbacy it came into Abbot Hugh's mind to go to the shrine of St. Thomas to pray; and on his way thither upon the day after the Nativity of the Virgin he had a grievous fall near Rochester, so that his knee-cap was put out and lodged in the ham of his leg. Physicians hastened to him and tortured him in many ways but healed him not; and he was carried back to us in a horse litter and devoutly received as was his due. To cut a long story short, his leg mortified and the pain ascended even to his heart, and by reason of the pain a tertian fever laid hold on him, in the fourth fit of which he died and gave up his soul to God on the morrow of the day of St. Brice. Before he died, everything was pillaged by his servants so that nothing was left in his house but three-legged stools and tables which they were unable to carry off. The Abbot himself was scarce left with his coverlet and two old torn blankets which someone had placed over him after removing those that were whole. There was nothing worth a single penny that could be distributed to the poor for the benefit of his soul. The Sacrist said that it was no business of his, asserting that he had found all expense for the Abbot and his household for a whole month. For the tenants of the townships refused to give anything before the appointed time and his creditors would lend him nothing, when they saw that he was sick even unto death. None the less the tenant of Palgrave found fifty shillings for distribution to the poor, since he entered on his tenancy of Palgrave on that day. But those fifty shillings were later given back to the King's bailiffs who demanded the whole rent on behalf of the King.

When Abbot Hugh had been buried, it was resolved in the Chapter that a messenger should announce his death to Ranulph de Glanvill, Justiciar of England. Master Samson and Master R. Ruff, monks of our house, crossed the sea and bore this news to our lord the King [Henry II]: and from him they secured letters to the effect that the property and revenues of the Convent, which were separated from those of the Abbot, should be wholly in the hands of the Prior and the Convent, while the rest of the Abbey should be in the hands of the King. The custody of the Abbey was given to Robert de Cockfield and Robert de Flamville, our Steward, who straightway placed under gage and pledge all the servants and kinsfolk of the Abbot, to whom he had given anything before he fell sick or who had taken anything from his property; and they did this even to the Abbot's chaplain, one of our monks, for whom the Prior stood security: and entering our vestry they caused an inventory to be made of all the ornaments of the church.

While the abbacy was vacant, we often besought God and his holy martyr, St. Edmund, as was meet and right, to give us a fitting shepherd for our Church, thrice every week prostrating ourselves in the choir after leaving the chapter house, and singing the seven penitential psalms; and some there were who, if they had known who was to be our Abbot, would not have prayed so devoutly. As to the choice of an Abbot, should the King grant us a free election, divers persons spoke in divers manners, some in public, some in private, and everyman had his own opinion. And one said of another, "That brother is a good monk, a person worthy of approval: he knows much concerning the Rule and the customs of the Church; though he be not so perfect a philosopher as certain others he might well fill the office of Abbot. Abbot Ording was an illiterate man, and yet he was a good Abbot and ruled this house wisely; moreover, we read in the Fables that it proved better for the frogs to choose a log for their king, in whom they could trust, than a serpent who hissed venomously and after hissing devoured his subjects." To this another made answer, "How may that be? How can he, a man who has no knowledge of letters, preach a sermon in Chapter, or on feast days to the people? How shall he who does not understand the Scriptures, have knowledge how to bind and how to loose? seeing that 'the rule of souls is the art of arts and the science of sciences.' God forbid that a dumb image should be set up in the Church of St. Edmund, where it is known that there are many men of learning and of industry." Again another said yet of another, "That brother is literate, eloquent and prudent, strict in his observance of the Rule; he has greatly loved the Convent, and has endured many ills for the possessions of the Church; he is worthy to be made Abbot." And another replied, "From all good clerks, O Lord deliver us; that it may please Thee to preserve us from all Norfolk barrators, we beseech Thee to hear us." Again one said of a certain brother, "That brother is a good manager, as is proved by the performance of his tasks and by the offices that he has filled so well, and the buildings and repairs that he has made. He knows how to work hard and to defend our house, and he is something of a clerk, though 'much learning maketh him not mad.' He is worthy to be Abbot." The other made answer, "God forbid that a man who cannot read or sing or celebrate the holy offices, a wicked man and unjust, a flayer of the poor—God forbid that such an one should be made Abbot!" Again a certain brother said of someone, "That brother is a kindly man, affable and amiable, peaceful and composed, bountiful and generous, a literate man and eloquent, a very proper man in aspect and bearing, who is loved by many both within and without. And such a man, God willing, might be made Abbot to the great honour of the Church." The other made answer, "Nay; it would be an onus rather than an honour to have such a man; for he is over nice about his food and drink, thinks it a virtue to sleep long, knows how to spend much and gain little, snores when others keep vigil, would always be in the midst of abundance and gives no thought to the debts that grow from day to day, nor to the expenditure, how it may be met; hating all toil and anxiety and caring for nought, provided that one day go and another come—a man that loves and cherishes flatterers and liars, and himself says one thing and does another. From such a ruler may the Lord defend us!" Again one said of his comrade, "That man is wiser almost than any of us, both in the things of the world and the things of the Church: a man of great wisdom, strict in observance of the Rule, literate and eloquent and personable in bearing. Such a ruler would beseem our Church." Another replied, "True, if only he were of sound and approved repute. But his reputation is deemed unsound, perhaps truly, perhaps falsely. And though he be a wise man, humble in Chapter, devout in the singing of Psalms, and strict in the cloister, while he is in the cloister, yet, if he chances to hold any office, he is apt to be disdainful, scorning monks and loving men of the world more than he should; and if he happen to be angry, he will not say a word in answer to any of the brethren, not even if he be asked a question." . . . Again another, who thought himself wise, said, "May God Almighty give us for our shepherd one who is a fool and ignorant, so that he will have to ask us to help him!" And I heard indeed that a certain man who was industrious and literate and of noble birth, was condemned by certain of our seniors because he was a novice, while the novices said of the seniors that they were decrepit old men, unfit to rule the Abbey. And so, many men said many things, and each of them "was fully persuaded in his own mind." I once saw Samson, the sub-sacrist, sitting by at gatherings of this kind at the time of blood-letting, when the cloister monks are wont to reveal the secrets of their hearts, each to each, and to confer with one another—I saw him sitting by and smiling, without a word, and noting the words of each; and I heard him repeat some of the aforesaid opinions after twenty years had passed. As he listened, I used to reply to those who passed judgment after this fashion, saying that if we had to wait to elect an Abbot until we found someone who was free of all blame and without spot, we should never find such an one, since no one lives wholly without censure, and "naught is in all things best." On one occasion I could not contain my spirit, but blurted out what I thought, thinking that I spoke to faithful ears, and I said that a certain brother was unworthy to be Abbot, though he had loved me and conferred many benefits upon me; and said I thought another of the sons of Belial revealed what I had said to my benefactor and friend: for which cause to this very day I have never either by prayer or gift been able to recover his favour to the full. What I have said I have said, and

> The word once spoken flieth past recall. . . .

After the death of Abbot Hugh, when a year and three months were gone, our lord the King sent letters to us, commanding that our Prior and twelve of the Convent, unanimously chosen by our whole body, should appear before him on an appointed day to elect an Abbot. On the day after we had received these letters, we assembled in the chapter house to deal with the matter. First of all the King's letters were read before the Convent: After this we asked the Prior and charged him on the peril of his soul to nominate according to his conscience the twelve whom he should take with him, men whose life and character made it clear that they would refuse to stray from the right way. And he, granting our petition and inspired by the Holy Spirit, chose six from one side of the choir and six from the other, and satisfied us, not a voice being raised against his choice. From the right side there were Geoffrey of Fordham, Benedict, Master Denys, Master Samson the sub-sacrist, Hugh the third Prior, and Master Hermer, at that time a novice; from the left William the Sacrist, Andrew, Peter of Brook, Roger the Cellarer, Master Ambrose, and Master Walter the physician. But one of us said, "What will happen, if those thirteen, when they come before the King, are unable to agree in their choice of an Abbot?" And one made answer, "This will be an everlasting reproach to us and to our Church." Therefore a number of us were for electing an Abbot at home before the others departed, in order that by thus taking forethought there might be no disagreement in the presence of the King. But it seemed to us to be foolish and unseemly to do this without the King's assent, since we did not yet know whether we should be able to secure a free election from our lord the King. Samson the sub-sacrist, speaking in the spirit, said, "Let us take a middle course that we may avoid peril on this side and on that. Let four confessors be chosen from the Convent and two from among the elder of our seniors, who are of good repute; and let them when they have looked upon the holy mysteries and laid their hands upon the Gospels, choose three men from the Convent whom they think best fitted for the office according to the Rule of St. Benedict; and let them set down the names in writing and enclose what they have written under seal; and thus enclosed, let it be consigned to those of us who are to go to the Court. And when we are come into the King's presence and have been assured of a free election, then at last let the seal be broken, and thus we shall ascertain who are the three whom we are to nominate before the King. If our lord the King refuse to grant us one of our own house, the seal shall be carried back unbroken, and handed to the six that have been sworn, so that their secret shall, on peril of their souls, be hidden for ever." To this counsel we all gave our assent: and four confessors were nominated, to wit Eustace, Gilbert of Elveden, Turstan and Ruald, both of them old men. This done, we went out singing

"Verba mea," and the aforesaid six remained behind, having the Rule of St. Benedict ready to hand; and thus they carried out the business according to their instructions. . . . But after some delay, the Convent returned to the chapter house; and the seniors said that they had done as they were bidden. Then the Prior asked what should be done if the King refused to accept any one of the three names that they had written; and he got the answer that we should accept anyone whom our lord the King was ready to accept, provided that he were a son of our church. And to this also was added that if these thirteen brethren saw anything in that writing that needed correction, they should alter it according to God's will, by the common assent or counsel of them all. Samson the sub-sacrist, who sat at the Prior's feet, said, "It is expedient for the sake of our Church that we should all swear upon the word of truth that, on whomsoever the choice should chance to fall, he should treat the Convent reasonably and refrain from changing obedientiaries without the consent of the Convent, or burdening the Sacrist or admitting any man as a monk without the good-will of the Convent." And this we all of us granted, raising our hands in token of assent. It was provided that if our lord the King should desire to make Abbot one who was not of our Church, he should not be accepted by the thirteen save with the counsel of the brethren who remained at home.

On the morrow therefore those thirteen set out upon their journey to the Court. Last of them all went Samson, who had charge of their expenses, because he was sub-sacristan. Hung about his neck he carried a case containing the letters of the Convent, as though he were the sole servant of them all; and without any to squire him, he went forth on his way to the Court, carrying his frock tucked up on his arms and following his comrades afar off. On the way to the Court, as the brethren talked together, Samson said that it would be well that all of them should swear that whosoever were made Abbot, he should give back the Churches of the Convent's domain to provide for the entertainment of guests, to which all gave their assent save only the Prior who said, "We have sworn enough: You may put such a burden on the Abbot that I for one should not care to have the abbacy." And so on this occasion they took no oath; and it was well done, because, if the oath had been sworn, it would not have been kept. On the same day that the thirteen departed from us, William of Hastings, one of our brethren, said as we sat in the cloister, "I know that we have one of our own folk as Abbot." And when he was asked how he knew this, he said that he had seen in a vision, as he slept, a prophet clad in white raiment standing before the gate of the monastery, and that he had asked him in the name of the Lord whether we should have one of ourselves for Abbot. And the prophet replied, "You shall have one of your own, but he shall raven among you like a wolf." And the purport of the dream was fulfilled in part since he that was to be Abbot was zealous to be feared rather than to be loved, as many of us said. And another brother was sitting with us, Edmund by name, who asserted that Samson would be Abbot, and told us of a vision that he had seen the night before. He said that he had seen Roger the Cellarer and Hugh the third prior standing before the altar, and between them was Samson, towering above them from the shoulders upwards and wearing a long cloak that flowed down to his heels and was bound around his shoulders, and he stood with raised fists ready for a fight. And St. Edmund rose from the feretory, as it seemed to him in his dreams and, as though some sickness was upon him, bared his feet and legs, and when someone drew near and would have covered his feet, the saint said, "Draw not near; behold that men shall veil my feet"; and he pointed with his finger towards Samson. Now this is the interpretation of the dream. In as much as he seemed like a fighter, it was foretold that the Abbot to be should live in toil, now contending with the Archbishop of Canterbury, concerning the pleas of the crown, now against the knights of St. Edmund concerning the payment of full scutage, now with the burgesses over encroachments in the market, now with the sokemen over the suits of the hundreds, wishing like a fighter to overcome his adversaries in battle, that he might reclaim the rights and liberties of this Church. As for the feet of the holy Martyr, he veiled them, when he completed the towers of the Church that were begun a hundred years before. Such were the dreams our brothers dreamed, which were forthwith bruited abroad, first through the cloister and next through the court, so that before evening it was said openly among the common people, "He and he and he have been chosen, and one of them will be Abbot."

But the Prior and the twelve with him, after much toil and delay, at length stood before the King at Waltham, a manor of the Bishop of Winchester, on the second Sunday in Lent. Our lord the King received them kindly and, declaring that he wished to act according to God's will and for the honour of the Church, he commanded the brethren by the mouth of his intermediaries, Richard Bishop of Winchester and Geoffrey the Chancellor, afterwards Archbishop of York, that they should nominate three of our Convent. Whereupon the Prior and the brethren went aside, as though to speak on this matter, and drew out the seal and broke it, and found the names in the following order: Samson the sub-sacrist, Roger the Cellarer and Hugh the third prior. Whereat the brothers who were of higher rank blushed. Moreover, all marvelled that the same Hugh was both elector and elect. But since they could not change the facts, by common consent they changed the order, putting Hugh first, because he was third prior, Roger the Cellarer second, and Samson third, making, on the face of it, the first last and the last first. But the King, after much enquiring whether those nominated were born in his realm and within whose domain, said that he did not know them and ordered that three others of the Convent should be nominated as well as those three. This being agreed, William the Sacrist said, "Our Prior should be nominated because he is our head." This was readily allowed. Then said the Prior, "William the Sacrist is a good man." The same was said of Denys, and it was allowed. These being nominated without delay before the King, he marvelled saying, "They have done this quickly; God is with them." Afterwards the King demanded that for the honour of his realm they should nominate three more from other houses. Hearing this the brethren were afraid, suspecting guile. At length they agreed to name three, but on this condition that they should accept none of them without the counsel of those of the Convent who remained at home. . . . This done, the King thanked them and gave orders that three out of the nine should be struck off the list, whereupon the three aliens were at once removed. . . . William the Sacrist withdrew of his own free will: two of the remaining five were struck off by order of the King, and then one of the three remaining, two only being left, namely the Prior and Samson. Finally the intermediaries of our lord the King whom I have mentioned above were called in to take counsel with the brethren. And Denys, speaking for us all, began to commend the persons of the Prior and Samson, saying that both were literate, both good, both of praiseworthy life and of unblemished reputation; but always in the corner of his speech thrusting Samson forward, multiplying the words he uttered in his praise and saying that he was a man strict in his behaviour, stern in chastising transgressions, a hard worker, prudent in worldly business, and proved in diverse offices. The Bishop of Winchester replied, "We understand clearly what you mean; from your words we gather that your Prior seems to you to be somewhat slack and that you desire him whom you call Samson." Denys replied, "Both of them are good, but we should like, God willing, to have the better." The Bishop made answer, "Of two good men you must choose the better. Tell me openly, do you wish to have Samson?" And a number, making a majority, answered clearly, "We want Samson," not a voice being raised against them, though some of set purpose said nothing because they wished to offend neither the one nor the other. Samson then having been nominated in the presence of the King, and the latter having taken brief counsel with his advisers, all the rest were summoned and the King said, "You have presented Samson to me: I do not know him. If you had presented your Prior, I should have accepted him; for I have seen him and I know him. But, as it is, I will do what you desire. But have a care; for by the very eyes of God, if you do ill, I will be at you!" He then asked the Prior, if he agreed to this and desired it. The Prior answered that he did desire it and that Samson was much more worthy of honour. The elect therefore fell at the King's feet and kissed them, then rose in haste, and in haste went to the altar with the brethren, singing "Miserere mei, Deus," his head held high and his countenance unchanged. And when the King saw this, he said to those who stood by, "By God's eyes, this elect thinks himself worthy to be the guardian of his Abbey." When the news of this election reached the Convent, it gladdened all the cloister monks, or nearly all, and certain of the obedientiaries, but only a few. "It is well," said many, "because it is well." Others said, "Nay, in truth we have all been deceived." The elect, before he returned to us, received his benediction from the lord Bishop of Winchester, who at the same time placed the mitre on his head and the ring upon his finger, saying, "This is the dignity of the Abbots of St. Edmund: it is long since I knew this." The Abbot then, keeping three monks with him, sent all the rest home in advance, announcing that he would come to them on Palm Sunday, and charging some of them with the duty of providing all that was necessary for his feast. On his return journey a multitude of new kinsmen went to meet him, desiring to be taken into his service. But to all of them he made answer that he was content with the Prior's servants, and could not keep any others until he had consulted the Convent on the matter. But one knight he kept with him, an eloquent man and skilled in the law, not so much on account of his kinship, but for his usefulness, since he was accustomed to secular business. So being new in office he took him to be his helper in worldly disputes; for he had but now received the abbacy and was unused to such matters, as he himself protested, since before he became Abbot he was never in any place where gage and pledge were given. He was well received by the Convent on Palm Sunday with all due honour and a procession as well. . . .

A general summons having been issued, all the barons and knights and free men came to do homage to him on the fourth day of Easter. And lo and behold, Thomas de Hastings came with a great multitude of knights, bringing with him Henry his nephew, who was not yet a knight, and claiming the stewardship on his behalf together with all the customs as stated in his charter. To this the Abbot at once made answer, "Henry's rights I neither deny, nor wish to deny them. If he was able to serve me in person, I would give him all that is needful for the maintenance of ten men and eight horses in my court, as is stated in his charter. If you should present to me as his substitute, a steward who knows how to perform the duties of stewardship, I would accept him on the same terms as my predecessor granted to his steward on the day whereon he, the Abbot, was alive and dead, to wit, four horses and their appurtenances. But if you will not agree thereto, I place my plea before the King or his Chief Justice." This said, the matter was postponed. Afterwards there was presented to him a simple and ignorant steward, Gilbert by name; but before he accepted him, he said to his friends, "If there is any default in the King's justice through the ignorance of the steward, it is he not I that will be accountable to the King, since he claims the stewardship by hereditary right: and therefore I prefer to accept him for the time being rather than take one who may be more skilled to deceive me. God helping, I will be my own steward."

After he had received homage, the Abbot demanded an aid from his knights, who promised him twenty shillings each; but they had no sooner done so than they took counsel together and withdrew twelve pounds in respect of twelve knights, saying that those twelve ought to help the other forty in respect of castleward and scutages and likewise of aids to the Abbot. When the Abbot heard this, he was angry and said to his friends that, if he lived, he would render them like for like, and trouble for trouble. After this the Abbot caused an inquiry to be made as to the annual rents due from the free men in each manor and as to the names of the peasants and their holdings and the services due from each; and he had them all set down in writing. But he restored old halls and ruinous houses, through which kites and crows were flying; he built new chapels and lodgings and chambers in many places, where there had never before been buildings save only barns. He also made a number of parks which he filled with beasts, and kept a huntsman and hounds; and when any distinguished guest came to him, he would sit at times with his monks in some woodland glade and watch the hounds run; but I never saw him taste venison. He also cleared many lands and brought them back into cultivation, but would that he had shown like zeal and vigilance in his bestowal of the manors of the Convent. None the less he took our manors of Bradfield and Rougham into his own hands for the time being, making good the deficit in the rent by the expenditure of forty pounds; these manors he afterwards returned to us, having heard that there were murmurs in the Convent because he kept our manors in his own hands. Also to rule these same manors and all others, he appointed both monks and laymen who were wiser than their former wardens, that they might make more prudent provision for ourselves and our lands. He kept eight hundreds in his own hands, and after the death of Robert de Cockfield he recovered the hundred of Cosford—all of which hundreds he handed over to the custody of his sergeants who ate at his own board, keeping the more important questions for himself and settling those of lesser importance through the agency of others, and turning everything to his own profit. At his bidding a general inventory was made, in each hundred, of leets and suits, hidages and corn-dues, payments of hens, and other customs, revenues and expenses, which had hitherto been largely concealed by the tenants: and he had all these things set down in writing, so that within four years from his election there was not one who could deceive him concerning the revenues of the Abbey to a single pennyworth, and this although he had not received anything in writing from his predecessors concerning the administration of the Abbey, save for one small sheet containing the names of the manors and the rent due from each tenancy. Now this book, in which were also recorded the debts which he had paid off, he called his Kalendar, and consulted it almost every day, as though he could see therein the image of his own efficiency as in a mirror.

On the first day on which he held a Chapter, he confirmed to us with his new seal sixty shillings from Southrey, which his predecessors had unjustly taken for themselves, having received it in the first instance from Edmund, styled "the golden monk," that he might hold the said township all the days of his life. And he issued an edict that henceforth no man should pledge any of the ornaments of the church without the consent of the Convent, as was commonly done, and that no charter should be sealed with the seal of the Convent save in Chapter in the presence of the Convent. And he made Hugh sub-sacrist, giving orders that William the Sacrist should do nothing in the sacristy in respect either of revenues or expenses, save with his assent. After this, but not on the same day, he transferred the former guardians of the oblations to other offices. And last of all he deposed William himself; whereat some who loved William said, "Behold the Abbot! Behold the wolf of the dream! Behold how he ravens!" and some wished to make a conspiracy against the Abbot. But this being revealed to the Abbot, since he did not wish to keep wholly silent on the matter nor yet to disquiet the Convent, he entered the Chapter on the morrow, drawing forth a bag full of cancelled bonds, with their seals still hanging from them, to wit, bonds given some by his predecessor, some by the Prior, some by the Sacrist, and some by the Chamberlain and other officials—the total amounting to three thousand and fifty-two pounds and one mark, all of capital alone apart from the accumulated interest, the amount of which could never be determined. For all these bonds he had come to terms within a year of his election, and within twelve years he had paid them all. "Behold," he said, "the wisdom of your Sacrist William! Behold all these bonds sealed with his seal, in which he had pledged silken copes, dalmatics, silver thuribles and Gospels bound in gold, without leave of the Convent; and all these things I have redeemed and restored to you." And he added much else to show why he had deposed William; but the chief cause he did not mention, not wishing to make a scandal of him. And when he had appointed Samson the Precentor in his place, a man who pleased all of us and was beyond all blame, all was peace again. But the Abbot caused the houses of the Sacristan in the cemetery to be razed to the ground, as being unworthy to stand upon the earth, on account of the frequent wine-bibbing and other things of which it is best to say nothing, which willy-nilly he had witnessed when he was sub-sacrist; and so he ordered all to be levelled to the ground, so that within a year, in the place where a fine building had stood, we saw beans sprouting, and nettles in abundance where once had lain jars of wine. . . .

At that time there came unexpected news of the death of the wife of Herlewin of Runcton, who had a charter granting her the tenancy of that township for her life time: and the Abbot said, "Yesterday I would have given sixty marks to free that manor; but now the Lord hath freed it." And having come thither without delay and taken the township into his own hands, he went on the morrow to Tilney, a part of that manor; and there a knight came to him offering him thirty marks if he might hold that carucate of land with its appurtenances, on terms of the ancient service, to wit, four pounds: but the Abbot refused him, and that year he got twenty-five pounds and the next year twenty from the land. This happening and the like made him hold everything in his own hand, even as we read elsewhere that "Caesar was everything." But he was no sluggard, and began before all else to build barns and byres: and he was more especially eager to cultivate his lands with profit, and was also vigilant in looking after his woods, concerning the granting or diminishing of which he confessed himself most avaricious. One sole manor, that of Thorp, he confirmed by charter to a certain Englishman, an adscript to the soil, in whose faithfulness he had all the greatest confidence, because he was a good farmer and could speak French.

Abbot Samson was of middle height, and almost entirely bald; his face was neither round or long, his nose prominent, his lips thick, his eyes clear as crystal and of penetrating glance; his hearing of the sharpest; his eyebrows grew long and were often clipped; a slight cold soon made him grow hoarse. On the day of his election he was forty-seven years old, and had been a monk for seventeen. He had a few white hairs in a red beard and a very few in the hair of his head, which was black and rather curly; but within fourteen years of his election he was white as snow. He was a man of extreme sobriety, never given to sloth, extremely strong and ever ready to go either on horseback or on foot, until old age prevailed and tempered his eagerness. When he heard of the capture of the Cross and the fall of Jerusalem, he began to wear drawers of haircloth, and a shirt of hair instead of wool, and to abstain from flesh and meat; none the less he desired that meat should be placed before him when he sat at table, that so our alms might be increased.[9] He preferred fresh milk and honey and the like to any other food. He hated liars and drunkards and wordy fellows, since virtue loves itself and hates its opposite. He condemned those who murmur at their food and drink, especially if they were monks, and preserved the old way of life that he had followed as a cloister monk; but he had this virtue, that he never liked to have a dish changed when it had once been placed before him. When I was a novice, I wished to try if this were true and, chancing to be a server in the refectory, I thought in my heart that I would place before him a dish, which displeased all the rest, on a platter that was very black and broken. And when he saw this, he was as one that saw not. But after a time I repented that I had done this, and forthwith seizing the platter, I changed both dish and platter for the better and carried them away; but he was angry and vexed and took the improvement ill. He was eloquent both in French and Latin, having regard rather to the sense of what he had to say than to ornaments of speech. He read English perfectly, and used to preach in English to the People, but in the speech of Norfolk, where he was born and bred, and to this end he ordered a pulpit to be set up in the church for the benefit of his hearers and as an ornament to the church. The Abbot seemed also to love the active life better than the contemplative; he had more praise for good obedientiaries than for good cloister monks; and rarely did he approve of any man solely for his knowledge of literature, unless he were also wise in worldly affairs. And when he heard of any prelate that he grew faint beneath the burden of his pastoral cares and turned anchorite, he did not praise him for so doing. He was loath to bestow much praise on kindly men, for he said, "He that seeks to please everyone, ought to please nobody." So in the first year of his abbacy he regarded all flatterers with hatred, especially if they were monks. But in process of time he seemed more ready to give ear to them and to be more friendly toward them. Wherefore it came to pass that, when a certain brother skilled in this art kneeled before him, and under pretense of giving him some good advice, had poured the oil of flattery into his ears, I laughed softly as I stood afar off: but when the monk retired, he called me and asked me why I laughed, and I replied that it was because the world was full of flatterers. To which the Abbot made answer, "My son, it is long since I have been acquainted with flatterers, and it is therefore that I cannot help listening to them. In many things I must feign, and in many I must dissemble, to maintain peace in the Convent. I shall not cease to listen to their words, but they will not deceive me, as they deceived my predecessor who was so foolish as to put faith in their counsels, so that long before his death neither he nor his household had ought to eat save what was borrowed from their creditors." . . . And in truth the Abbot was at pains to have his house well disciplined and a household that, although large, was all of it necessary, and he made provision for himself so that the weekly sum, which had served his predecessor only for the expenses of five days, served him for eight, or nine, or ten, if he was away at his manors and there was no large arrival of guests. And every week he heard the account of his expenditure, not by deputy, but in person, which had never been the custom of his predecessor. During the first seven years of his abbacy, four dishes were served to him, but afterwards only three, except when he had received presents or venison from his parks or fish from his ponds. And if perchance he kept any man in his household at the request of some person of importance or some familiar friend, or maintained messengers or harpers or any such persons, as soon as he had an opportunity to go overseas or on a long journey, he prudently discarded such burdensome superfluities. As for the monks who had been his comrades before he succeeded to the abbacy, and had stood high in his love and regard, he rarely promoted them to office on the strength of his former affection, unless they were fit; wherefore some of our brethren, who had favored his election as Abbot, said that he showed less regard than was seemly toward those who had loved him before he was Abbot, and that he loved those better who had both openly and in secret disparaged him and had publicly and even in the hearing of many called him an angry and unsociable man, a haughty fellow and a barrator [10] from Norfolk. But as after his succession of the abbacy, he vouchsafed no indiscreet affection or honour to those who had once been his friends, even so he showed no sign of rancour or hatred to others, such as their conduct might seem to deserve, sometimes rendering good for evil and doing good to those who had persecuted him. He also had a habit, which I have never marked in any other man, namely, that he warmly loved many toward whom he never or rarely showed a loving countenance, nor conformed to the proverb "Where your love is, there your eye is also." And he had another characteristic that calls for wonder, namely, that he wittingly put up with losses in temporal matters at the hands of his servants, and acknowledged that he did so;

but to my thinking the reason was this, that he might wait for a suitable occasion to set matters right with greater prudence or that by shutting his eyes to the offense he might avoid great loss.

NOTES TO CHAPTER II

1. Roger of Wendover, from *The Flowers of History*, vol. 2, ed. J. A. Giles (London: G. Bell & Sons, 1849), p. 6. Reprinted by permission of the publisher.
2. From *The Mirror of Charity*, trans. and arr. Geoffrey Webb and Adrian Walker (London: A. R. Mowbray & Co., 1962), p. 118. Reprinted by permission of the publisher.
3. *Medieval Panorama: The English Scene from Conquest to Reformation* (Cambridge University Press, 1938; reprint ed., New York: Meridian Books, 1955), p. 266.
4. *Church, Kingship and Lay Investiture in England, 1089-1135* (Princeton, N.J.: Princeton University Press, 1958), p. 254.
5. While Anselm was in voluntary exile in France, King Henry sent William, bishop of Rouen, to Rome to negotiate. William apparently was instrumental in persuading the pope to offer a compromise settlement.
6. *The Centenary Edition of the Works of Thomas Carlyle* (New York: Charles Scribners, n.d.), 10:41.
7. Dom. David Knowles, *The Monastic Orders in England, 943-1216* (Cambridge: Cambridge University Press, 1950), pp. 306-7.
8. Quoted by J. C. Dickson, *Monastic Life in Medieval England* (New York: Barnes and Noble, 1962), p. 100.
9. The uneaten food from the monastery table was given to the poor.
10. A deceitful lawyer.

CHAPTER III

The Life of the Feudal Aristocracy

THE ARISTOCRACY OF Norman England retained the Saxon and Norse ideals of courage and loyalty which are illustrated in the story of the battle of Maldon. Feudalism, however, represented a more complex society, and the feudal knight came to value other virtues as well. Encouraged by the minstrels, who glorified his deeds and sought his support, the knight laid emphasis on another Germanic ideal, generosity. He also came to value courtesy, respect for a code of behavior governing his conduct toward fellow aristocrats, even if they were enemies. In time the term "knight" came to mean more than merely a mounted warrior; knighthood took on the attributes of a kind of lay order. During the century following the first crusade (1095), religious authors, such as John of Salisbury, stressed the Christian knight's obligation to defend the faith and serve the church.[1]

According to contemporary accounts, many English leaders of the period possessed chivalric virtues. William of Malmesbury depicts Robert earl of Gloucester (Matilda's leader against Stephen) as valiant and generous, while another chronicler relates how King Stephen personally led his troops across a deep ford: "He most gallantly plunged in himself among the foremost, swiftly made his way across by swimming rather than wading, furiously charged the enemy, and compelling them to retreat to the gates of the city (Oxford), joined battle with them with greatest spirit." [2] But despite their chivalric ideals, the feudal aristocracy were contentious, irresponsible, and often ruthless. As a king, Stephen proved a failure. The same chronicler admits that during his reign England became "a haunt of strife, a training ground of disorder, and a teacher of every kind of rebellion. The sacred obligations of friendship were at once broken among the people, the closest bonds of relationship were loosened. . . . For each man, seized by a strange passion for violence, raged cruelly against his neighbour and reckoned himself the more glorious the more guiltily he attacked the innocent." [3]

Feudalism, though it developed a legal code based on contractual relationships, could not provide an ordered society. Only a strong monarch like Henry II could restrain the disastrous particularism of aristocratic rule. A chivalric king like Richard the Lionhearted could instill loyalty among his immediate followers, as is described in the following selection from Richard of Devizes, but under him and his successor, John, the barons threatened to disrupt the kingdom. Yet, if unable to govern effectively, the aristocracy made an important contribution to the country's constitutional growth: they checked royal absolutism. The account below of the battle of Bouvines and of the events leading up to the signing of the Great Charter shows the military and political importance of the aristocracy at the opening of the 13th century.

At first the code of chivalry was purely masculine. The earliest popular story of the legend of King Arthur, Geoffrey of Monmouth's *History of the Kings of Britain* (early 12th century), pays little heed to women, but during the 12th century a romantic as well as a religious element was introduced. Robert of Gloucester is reputed to have remarked, "I serve Venus as a volunteer, but fight for Mars only when I must."[4] By 1200, romances, sung by trouvères and troubadours from France, vied in popularity with warlike epics. While romances still extolled the warrior ideals, their central theme was love. The last two selections in this chapter are two such romances.

Richard of Devizes's Chronicle of King Richard the Lionhearted (1190)

The following account of Richard's seizure of Messina in 1190 shows the persistence of the warrior concept of leadership and loyalty, the kind of attitude toward the fighting group which Lionel Tiger believes has been characteristic of warfare since primitive society.[5] In the story Richard appears in the heroic role of rallying his men against great odds; but he did not fight solely to defend the honor of the English. Tancred, the natural son of a former king, had just been elected by the anti-imperial faction in Sicily to succeed his cousin William II. Since William II had been married to Richard's sister, the English king demanded her return, not only with her dowry but also with a treasure which William II had reputedly willed to Henry II of England. Both Richard and his great rival, King Philip of France, had stopped in Sicily on their way to the Holy Land. Richard took advantage of his sojourn to force his demands on Tancred. Philip stood by without interfering, then asked to share in the proceeds. Thus, if from one angle the following is a chivalric tale of valor, from another it may seem a story of blackmail and bribery.

Richard of Devizes, the author, was a monk of Saint Swithin's in Winchester. His chronicle covers the years from Richard's coronation in 1189 until the king's preparations to leave the Holy Land in 1192.

King Richard's Battle with the Sicilians

Before the arrival of King Richard in Sicily, the Griffons were stronger than all the other rulers of that region.[6] While they had always hated the Ultramontanes, now, irritated by fresh injuries, they burned more fiercely than ever. They made peace with all who recognized the king of France as lord, and then they sought full revenge for their injuries from the king of the English and his tail-bearing men. (The paltry Greeks and Sicilians called all those who followed that king "Englishmen" and "tailed.") The English, therefore, were denied all trade with the country by edict, and they were slain both by day and by night by forties and fifties, wherever they were found unarmed. The slaughter increased every day, and it was planned to continue with this madness till every one of them was either killed or put to flight. The king of England, that fearful lion, was aroused by these tumults and roared horribly, burning with a rage worthy of such a beast. His raving fury terrified his dearest friends. The court drew together. The designated leaders of the army sat round the throne, each in his place; and one might very easily read in the ruler's face what he was silently considering in his mind, if anyone had dared lift his eyes to the king's face. After a long and profound silence, the king expressed his indignation thus: "O my soldiers, the strength and crown of my realm!

You have endured a thousand perils with me; you who by your bravery have conquered so many kings and cities for me, do you not see that the cowardly mob is now insulting us? Will we overcome Turks and Arabs, will we be the terror of the most invincible nations, will our right arms make a way for us to the ends of the earth after the Cross of Christ, will we restore the kingdom of Israel, if we show our backs to these vile and effeminate Griffons? If we are defeated here in the confines of our own country, will we go any farther? Shall the laziness of Englishmen be made a joke to the ends of the world? My men, is not this new cause of grief to me a very just one? It may be, I think, that you are deliberately sparing your strength now, so that perhaps later on you may fight more boldly against Saladin.

"I, your lord and your king, love you. I am solicitous for your good name. I tell you and I repeat that if by chance you go away from here without your revenge, the base repute of this flight will go ahead of you and accompany you. Old women and little children will rise up against you, and boldness will give a double strength to the enemies of men who have run away. I know that he who keeps a man against his will does the same as kill him. The king will keep no man against his will. I do not want to force anyone to stay with me, lest one man's fear in battle might destroy another's confidence. Let each man follow the course he chooses, but as for me, I will either die here or get revenge for my injuries, which are your injuries, too. If I go away from here alive, Saladin will not see me unless I am victorious. If you flee, you will leave me, your king, whom you will have deserted, to face the danger alone."

The king had scarcely finished his speech when all the brave men roared, disturbed only by the fact that their lord seemed not to trust his men. They promised from their hearts to be ready to do whatever he ordered, ready to scale mountains and to break through walls of bronze. Let him lay aside his frown; they would make all Sicily subject to him by their sweat, if he so ordered.

They would all wade to the Pillars of Hercules in blood, if he so desired.

When the noise was hushed by the ruler's authority, "What I hear pleases me," he said. "You gladden my heart, you who are ready to cast away your disgrace. And, because it is always harmful to put things off when they are ready, there must be no delay, so that what we are going to do may be done quickly. First, you must capture Messina for me. Then the Griffons shall either ransom themselves or be sold into slavery. If King Tancred does not make speedy satisfaction for my sister's dower and King William's legacy, which falls to me as my father's heir, after his kingdom has been depopulated he shall be compelled to pay everything four times over. Booty shall belong to whoever takes it in battle. Perfect peace is to be observed only towards my lord, the king of the French, who is taking his rest in the city, and all his men. Within two days let about 2,000 knights, chosen from the whole army, men whose hearts are not in their boots, and 1,000 archers on foot make ready. Let the law be observed without any exceptions. Whoever runs away on foot shall lose a foot. A knight shall be stripped of his belt. Let each man be in his proper place in the battle array according to military discipline, and on the third day, at the sound of the trumpet, let each man follow me into the city, and I will go first and show the way." The council broke up with great applause, and the king, his stern expression gone, seemed to thank them for their goodwill by the very serenity of his countenance.

It wonderfully came to pass that even his enemies could not allege that the king's cause was unjust. On the third day, when the army was to have been led forth, early in the morning, Richard, archbishop of Messina, the archbishop of Monreale, the archbishop of Reggio, the Admiral Margarito, Jordan of Pin, and many other friends of King Tancred, taking with them Philip, king of the French, the bishop of Chartres, the duke of Burgundy, the counts of Nevers and Perche, and many followers of the king of France, as well as the archbishops of Rouen and Auch, the bishops of Evreux and Bayonne, and everyone who was thought to have some influence with the English, came respectfully to the king of England to make satisfaction to him for all his complaints, according to his pleasure. The king, after being long and earnestly entreated, yielded to the persistency of so many men and left the terms of the peace to the suitors themselves. Let them consider what he had put up with, he said, and let them see to it that the terms of the treaty were no lighter than the wrongs he had suffered. He would be satisfied with whatever their deliberations should decide to be due, if only from that very moment none of the Griffons should lay hands on his men, now or in the future. Those who had come were greatly surprised and even more delighted at the unhoped-for mildness of his reply, and agreeing to what he had last proposed, they sat down together to deal with the rest, away from the king's presence.

The king's army, numbered off the day before, had been waiting for the herald in solemn silence outside the camp since sunrise, and the peacemakers, proceeding in a dilatory fashion, had drawn out their negotiations till fully the third hour of the day, when behold! suddenly and unexpectedly a loud voice outside the gates cried: "To arms, to arms, men! Hugh the Brown has been seized and is being killed by the Griffons, his belongings are being plundered, and his men are being slain." [7] The cry that the peace had been broken threw the negotiators into confusion, and the king of France exclaimed: "I am convinced that God hates these men and has hardened their hearts, so that they may fall into the hands of the torturer!" He went quickly with all who were with him to the king's tent and found him already putting on his armour. He said to him in a few words: "I will be a witness before all men that, whatever may happen, you will be blameless if you now take up arms against the damned Griffons."

He spoke and withdrew. Those who had come with him followed him and were received with him into the city.

The king of England went forth armed; the terrible dragon standard was carried before him unfurled; and the army moved after him at the sound of a trumpet. The sun glistened on golden shields, and the mountains shone brightly with the reflection from them. They went forth carefully and in good order, and the business was done without any foolishness.

The Griffons, on the other side, locked the gates of the city and stood in arms at the ramparts of the walls and towers, fearing nothing as yet, and shot at the army incessantly. The king, who knew nothing better than storming cities and overthrowing castles, first let them empty their quivers. Then at length he made the first assault by his bowmen, who went in front of the army. The sky was hidden by a violent rain of arrows; a thousand darts pierced the shields extended along the ramparts; and nothing could save the rebels from the force of the javelins. The walls were left without guards, for no-one could look out without getting an arrow in his eye immediately. In the meantime the king, with his army, came up to the gates of the city unopposed, freely, and as it were, without restraint. When the battering ram was moved up, he broke down the gates more quickly than it takes to tell about it. He led the army into the city and captured all the fortified places up to Tancred's palace and the quarters of the French around their king's lodging, which he spared out of respect for his lord the king. The victors' banners were placed on the towers of the city in a circle. He turned over the captured fortifications to the leaders of the army, one to each, and he made his nobles take up quarters in the city. He took as hostages the sons of all the nobles of the city and the province, so that either they might be ransomed according to the king's evaluation of them or else the remainder of the city might be given up to him without a struggle and his demands from its king, Tancred, might be satisfied. He began the assault of the city at the fifth hour of the day and took it on the tenth hour. Then he recalled his army and returned victorious to the camp. King Tancred, terrified when the news of the outcome of the engagement was brought to him, hastened to make a settlement with him. He sent him 20,000 ounces of gold for his sister's dower and another 20,000 ounces of gold as King William's legacy and to ensure the observance of a perpetual peace with him and his subjects. That small sum of money was received very reluctantly and indignantly; the hostages were returned, and a firm peace was sworn to by the great men on both sides.

The king of England, as yet trusting the natives very little, built a new stronghold of wood of great strength and height near the walls of Messina. As a taunt to the Griffons, he called it "The Griffon-Killer." The king's valour was greatly glorified, and "all the earth kept silent before him."

Roger of Wendover's Account of the Battle of Bouvines and the Signing of Magna Carta (1216)

Sidney Painter, author of an outstanding study of King John, concludes that there is "no justification for calling John a tyrant in the political or constitutional sense."[8] Instead, Painter sees him as a much better administrator than either his brother Richard I or his son Henry III. He ran into opposition primarily because he sought to continue the policy of increasing royal power. Still, Painter admits that the deficiencies of his personal character—his cruelty, deceitfulness, and suspicious nature—helped to unite his enemies and stir them to action.

In 1213 John hoped to reestablish the power of the monarchy despite his earlier misfortunes. Having made peace with Pope Innocent III, he planned to recover Normandy from Philip with the assistance of the count of Flanders and Emperor Otto. To finance his expedition to France he collected money by every possible means, thereby arousing new opposition in England.

Philip checked his advance in western France, while the earl of Salisbury and his allies met decisive defeat at Bouvines. John had to return empty-handed to England late in 1214 to face his opponents. By the next June he realized he must agree to their proposals for a charter of liberties modeled after that of Henry I.

By John's time royal armies, such as that led by Salisbury at Bouvines, no longer consisted of feudal levies. The crown now normally demanded money payments (scutage) instead of knights' service from its vassals and employed largely mercenary troops. The growth of a money economy had undermined feudalism, but had not destroyed it. The baronial class still provided the military leaders and kings, like John and Philip, and sometimes granted annual incomes to vassals in return for homage, fealty, and military service, thus preserving the feudal relationship in a modified form.[9] The barons retained considerable military and political influence. Without their material support the king could not carry on an effective government.

The significance of Magna Carta has been the subject of much debate. Since the barons who forced it on John were concerned with defining and defending their feudal liberties, some of its provisions are reactionary. Article Sixty-one (included below) especially reveals how limited a concept of the state the feudal aristocracy actually held. Nevertheless, the charter contains clauses protecting others besides the aristocracy and the church. Above all, it expresses the principle that the king is bound by law. As a specific program for immediate reform it proved ineffective. "It was in the three centuries that elapsed after 1215, when it was thrice revised and many times confirmed, that Magna Carta gained its real significance. It had once and for all superseded the vague laws of Edward the Confessor as the criterion of good government." [10]

Roger of Wendover was the first of a series of monks at Saint Albans who composed a detailed chronicle of English history during the 13th and 14th centuries. Internal evidence suggests that Wendover began writing about 1216, so his account of Magna Carta is not strictly contemporary but reflects opinions just after the death of John. His sympathies are obviously with the baronial party.[11]

The Battle of Bouvines and the Signing of Magna Carta

How the king of the French marched against the army of the English king in Flanders.

At this time the English king's army in Flanders had spread its ravages through several provinces, and was now laying waste Poictou in a most relentless manner; in this expedition were the warlike and tried men William duke of Holland; Reginald, formerly count of Boulogne; Ferrand count of Flanders; and Hugh de Boves, a brave soldier though a cruel and proud man, for he showed his cruel disposition in those regions by sparing neither the female sex nor the young children. King John had appointed his brother William earl of Salisbury, marshal over that army, and over the knights of the kingdom, to fight in conjunction with them, and also to give the pay from the treasury to the other soldiers. These warriors were moreover assisted and favoured by Otho the Roman emperor, with all the forces of the dukes of Louvaine and Brabant, who were equally exasperated against the French. When all these proceedings came to the knowledge of Philip king of the French, he was much alarmed lest he should be unable to defend that part of the country, having lately sent his son Louis with a large army into Poictou to oppose the English king, and to check his hostile incursions there; and although the said king often thought on the common proverb—

"Whose mind to many schemes is bent,
On each can scarcely be intent."

He however collected an army of earls, barons, knights, and soldiers, horse and foot, together with the commoners of the cities and towns, and advanced in great force to meet his enemies, giving orders to the priests, religious men, clerks and nuns, to give alms, to offer prayers to God, and to perform services for the firm standing of his kingdom; after which he boldly marched with his army against the enemy. Hearing that the latter had already arrived as far as the bridge of Bovines in the territory of Pontoise, he led his forces in that direction, and arriving at the aforesaid bridge, he crossed the river with his army, and there pitched his camp. The heat of the sun was very great, as is usual in the month of July, on which account the French determined to halt near the river for the sake of refreshing the men as well as the horses. They arrived at the before-mentioned river on a Saturday, about the hour of evening; and, having arranged the carts, waggons, and all the vehicles in which they conveyed their food and arms, engines of war and weapons; to the right and left they appointed watches all round, and rested there for the night. When morning came, and the English commanders were informed that the French king had arrived, they held a council, and unanimously determined to give open battle to the enemy; but, as it was Sunday, it seemed to the more prudent men of the army, and especially to Reginald, formerly count of Boulogne, that it was improper to engage in battle on such a festival, and to profane such a day by slaughter and the effusion of human blood. The Roman emperor Otho coincided in this opinion, and said that he had never gained a triumph on such a day; on hearing this Hugh de Boves broke forth into blasphemy, calling count Reginald a base traitor, and reproaching him with the lands and large possessions he had received as gifts from the king of England; he added also that, if the battle was put off that day, it would redound to the irreparable loss of king John, for "delays are always dangerous when things are ready." But count Reginald, in reply to the taunts of Hugh, said indignantly, "This day will prove me faithful, and you the traitor;

for even on this very Sunday, if necessary, I will stand up in battle for the king, even to the death, and you, according to your custom, will, by fleeing from the battle show yourself a most base traitor in the presence of all." By these and other abusive words of the said Hugh, the whole multitude were stirred up and excited to battle; they therefore all flew to arms and boldly prepared for fighting. When all were armed, they arranged themselves in three bodies, over the first of which they appointed Ferrand count of Flanders, Reginald earl of Boulogne, and William earl of Salisbury, as commanders; the command of the third was assigned to Otho the Roman emperor and his fighting men; and in this manner they slowly marched forth against the enemy, and arrived in sight of the French army. When the French king saw that his enemies were prepared for a pitched battle, he ordered the bridge in his rear to be broken down, that, in case any of his army would endeavour to fly, they should have no where to fly except amongst the enemy. The French king having drawn up his troops, surrounded by his waggons and other vehicles, as already mentioned, there awaited the assault of his enemies. In short, the battalions commanded by the above-named counts burst upon the ranks of the French with such impetuosity, that in a moment they broke their ranks, and forced their way even up to where the French king was. Count Reginald, when he saw the king who had disinherited him and expelled him from his county, couched his lance against him, and having forced him to the ground, was preparing to slay him with his sword; but one of the soldiers, who had been appointed as a body-guard for the king, exposed himself to the blows of the count and was killed in his stead. The French, seeing their king on the ground, rushed impetuously and in great force to his assistance, and re-mounted him on his horse; then the battle raged on both sides, swords glistened like lightning around helmeted heads, and the conflict was most severe on both sides. The before-mentioned counts with the body of troops under their command had become separated from the rest of their fellow soldiers, and their retreat, as well as the advance of the rest of the army to their succour, was stopped; and thus their small body not being able to withstand the attacks of such numbers of the French, at length gave way, and in this manner the aforesaid counts with the whole of the band which they commanded, were, after showing great bravery, taken and made prisoners. . . .

The king of the French, in his joy for such unexpected victory, gave thanks to God for having granted him such a triumph over his enemies. The three counts above named, with a great number of knights and others, were taken away to be imprisoned. The battle took place on the 27th of July. By this misfortune the English king ineffectually spent the forty thousand marks which he had taken from the monks of the Cistercian order during the time of the interdict, thus verifying the proverb,

"Inglorious spoil will never end in good."

When at length the news of this event came to king John's knowledge he was thrown into dismay, and said to those about him, "Since I became reconciled to God, and submitted myself and my kingdoms to the church of Rome, woe is me, nothing has gone prosperously with me, and every thing unlucky has happened to me." . . .

Of a truce made between the French and English kings.

After the events above-mentioned, by the intervention of religious men, a truce was agreed on in the transmarine provinces between Philip and John, the French and English kings. . . . On the 19th of October, king John, having settled all his business in the transmarine provinces, returned home to England.

Of a conference held by the barons against king John.

About this time the earls and barons of England assembled at St. Edmund's, as if for religious duties, although it was for some other reason; for after they had discoursed together secretly for a time, there was placed before them the charter of king Henry the First, which they had received, as mentioned before, in the city of London from Stephen [Langton] archbishop of Canterbury. This charter contained certain liberties and laws granted to the holy church as well as to the nobles of the kingdom, besides some liberties which the king added of his own accord. All therefore assembled in the church of St. Edmund, the king and martyr, and, commencing from those of the highest rank, they all swore on the great altar that, if the king refused to grant these liberties and laws, they themselves would withdraw from their allegiance to him, and make war on him, till he should, by a charter under his own seal, confirm to them every thing they required; and finally it was unanimously agreed that, after Christmas, they should all go together to the king and demand the confirmation of the aforesaid liberties to them, and that they should in the meantime provide themselves with horses and arms, so that if the king should endeavour to depart from his oath, they might by taking his castles, compel him to satisfy their demands; and having arranged this, each man returned home.

King John held his court at Winchester at Christmas for one day, after which he hurried to London, and took up his abode at the New Temple; and at that place the above-mentioned nobles came to him in gay military array, and demanded the confirmation of the liberties and laws of king Edward, with other liberties granted to them and to the kingdom and church of England, as were contained in the charter, and above-mentioned laws of Henry the First; they also asserted that, at the time of his absolution at Winchester, he had promised to restore those laws and ancient liberties, and was bound by his own oath to observe them. The king, hearing the bold tone of the barons in making this demand, much feared an attack from them, as he saw that they were prepared for battle; he however made answer that their demands were a matter of importance and difficulty, and he therefore asked a truce till the end of Easter, that he might, after due deliberation, be able to satisfy them as well as the dignity of his crown. After much discussion on both sides, the king at length, although unwillingly, procured the archibishop of Canterbury, the bishop of Ely, and William Marshal, as his sureties, that on the day pre-agreed on he would, in all reason, satisfy them all, on which the nobles returned to their homes. The king however, wishing to take precautions against the future, caused all the nobles throughout England to swear fealty to him alone against all men, and to renew their homage to him; and, the better to take care of himself, he, on the day of St. Mary's purification, assumed the cross of our Lord, being induced to this more by fear than devotion.

Of the principal persons who compelled the king to grant the laws and liberties.

In Easter week of this same year, the above-mentioned nobles assembled at Stamford, with horses and arms; for they had now induced almost all the nobility of the whole kingdom to join them, and constituted a very large army; for in their army there were computed to be two thousand knights, besides horse soldiers, attendants, and foot soldiers, who were variously equipped. . . .

On the Monday next after the octaves of Easter, the said barons assembled in the town of Brackley; and when the king learned this, he sent the archbishop of Canterbury, and William Marshal earl of Pembroke, with some other prudent men, to them to inquire what the laws and liberties were which they demanded. The barons then delivered to the messengers a paper, containing in great measure the laws and ancient customs of the kingdom, and declared that, unless the king immediately granted them and confirmed them under his own seal, they would, by taking possession of his fortresses, force him to give them sufficient satisfaction as to their before-named demands. The archbishop with his fellow messengers then carried the paper to the king, and read to him the heads of the paper one by one throughout. The king when he heard the purport of these heads, derisively said, with the greatest indignation, "Why, amongst these unjust demands, did not the barons ask for my kingdom also? Their demands are vain and visionary, and are unsupported by any plea of reason whatever." And at length he angrily declared with an oath, that he would never grant them such liberties as would render him their slave. . . .

The castle of Northampton besieged by the barons.

As the archbishop and William Marshal could not by any persuasions induce the king to agree to their demands, they returned by the king's order to the barons, and duly reported all they had heard from the king to them; and when the nobles heard what John said, they appointed Robert Fitzwalter commander of their soldiers, giving him the title of "Marshal of the army of God and the holy church," and then, one and all flying to arms, they directed their forces towards Northampton. On their arrival there they at once laid siege to the castle, but after having stayed there for fifteen days, and having gained little or no advantage, they determined to move their camp; for having come without petrariae [catapults] and other engines of war, they, without accomplishing their purpose, proceeded in confusion to the castle of Bedford. At that siege the standard-bearer of Robert Fitz-Walter, among others slain, was pierced through the head with an arrow from a cross-bow and died, to the grief of many.

How the city of London was given up to the barons.

When the army of the barons arrived at Bedford, they were received with all respect by William de Beauchamp. There also came to them there messengers from the city of London, secretly telling them, if they wished to get into that city, to come there immediately. The barons, inspirited by the arrival of this agreeable message, immediately moved their camp and arrived at Ware; after this they marched the whole night, and arrived early in the morning at the city of London, and, finding the gates open, they, on the 24th of May, which was the Sunday next before our Lord's ascension, entered the city without any tumult while the inhabitants were performing divine service; for the rich citizens were favourable to the barons, and the poor ones were afraid to murmur against them. The barons having thus got into the city, placed their own guards in charge of each of the gates, and then arranged all matters in the city at will. They then took security from the citizens, and sent letters throughout England to those earls, barons, and knights, who appeared to be still faithful to the king, though they only pretended to be so, and advised them with threats, as they regarded the safety of all their property and possessions, to abandon a king who was perjured and who warred against his barons, and together with them to stand firm and fight against the king for their rights and for peace; and that, if they refused to do this, they, the barons, would make war against them all, as against open enemies, and would destroy their castles, burn their houses and other buildings, and destroy their warrens, parks, and orchards.

The conference between the king and the barons.

King John, when he saw that he was deserted by almost all, so that out of his regal superabundance of followers he scarcely retained seven knights, was much alarmed lest the barons would attack his castles and reduce them without difficulty, as they would find no obstacle to their so doing; and he deceitfully pretended to make peace for a time with the aforesaid barons, and sent William Marshal earl of Pembroke, with other trustworthy messengers, to them, and told them that, for the sake of peace, and for the exaltation and honour of the kingdom, he would willingly grant them the laws and liberties they required; he also sent word to the barons by these same messengers, to appoint a fitting day and place to meet and carry all these matters into effect. The king's messengers then came in all haste to London, and without deceit reported to the barons all that had been deceitfully imposed on them; they in their great joy appointed the fifteenth of June for the king to meet them, at a field lying between Staines and Windsor. Accordingly, at the time and place pre-agreed on, the king and nobles came to the appointed conference, and when each party had stationed themselves apart from the other, they began a long discussion about terms of peace and the aforesaid liberties. There were present on behalf of the king, the archbishops, Stephen of Canterbury, and H. of Dublin; the bishops W. of London, P. of Winchester, H. of Lincoln, J. of Bath, Walter of Worcester, W. of Coventry, and Benedict of Rochester; master Pandulph familiar of our lord the pope, and brother Almeric the master of the knights-templars in England; the nobles, William Marshal earl of Pembroke, the earl of Salisbury, earl Warrenne, the earl of Arundel, Alan de Galwey, W. Fitz-Gerald, Peter Fitz-Herbert, Alan Basset, Matthew Fitz-Herbert, Thomas Basset, Hugh de Neville, Hubert de Burgh seneschal of Poictou, Robert de Ropeley, John Marshal, and Philip d'Aubeny. Those who were on behalf of the barons it is not necessary to enumerate, since the whole nobility of England were now assembled together in numbers not to be computed. At length, after various points on both sides had been discussed, king John, seeing that he was inferior in strength to the barons, without raising any difficulty, granted the underwritten laws and liberties, and confirmed them by his charter as follows:—

Articles 61 and 63 of Magna Carta:

61. Since, moreover, for the sake of God, and for the improvement of our kingdom, and for the better quieting of the hostility sprung up lately between us and our barons, we have made all these concessions; wishing them to enjoy these in a complete and firm stability forever, we make and concede to them the security described below; that is to say, that they shall elect twenty-five barons of the kingdom, whom they will, who ought with all their power to observe, hold, and cause to be observed, the peace and liberties which we have conceded to them, and by this our present charter confirmed to them; in this manner, that if we or our

justiciar, or our bailiffs, or any one of our servants shall have done wrong in any way toward any one, or shall have transgressed any of the articles of peace or security; and the wrong shall have been shown to four barons of the aforesaid twenty-five barons, let those four barons come to us or to our justiciar, if we are out of the kingdom, laying before us the transgression, and let them ask that we cause that transgression to be corrected without delay. And if we shall not have corrected the transgression or, if we shall be out of the kingdom, if our justiciar shall not have corrected it within a period of forty days, counting from the time in which it has been shown to us or to our justiciar, if we are out of the kingdom; the aforesaid four barons shall refer the matter to the remainder of the twenty-five barons, and let these twenty-five barons with the whole community of the country distress and injure us in every way they can; that is to say by the seizure of our castles, lands, possessions, and in such other ways as they can until it shall have been corrected according to their judgment, saving our person and that of our queen, and those of our children; and when the correction has been made, let them devote themselves to us as they did before. And let whoever in the country wishes take an oath that in all the above-mentioned measures he will obey the orders of the aforesaid twenty-five barons, and that he will injure us as far as he is able with them, and we give permission to swear publicly and freely to each one who wishes to swear, and no one will we ever forbid to swear. . . .

63. Wherefore we will and firmly command that the Church of England shall be free, and that the men in our kingdom shall have and hold all the aforesaid liberties, rights and concessions, well and peacefully, freely and quietly, fully and completely, for themselves and their heirs, from us and our heirs, in all things and places, forever, as before said. It has been sworn, moreover, as well on our part as on the part of the barons, that all these things spoken of above shall be observed in good faith and without any evil intent. Witness the above named and many others. Given

by our hand in the meadow which is called Runnymede, between Windsor and Staines, on the fifteenth day of June, in the seventeenth year of our reign.

Two Medieval Romances
(12th Century)

The first of the two stories below, *The Lay of Milon,* is from a collection by a poetess of the 12th century known as Marie de France. Although she wrote in French, there is evidence that she was a subject of Henry II and may have lived in England. The second tale, *The Chatelaine of Vergi,* dates from the same period, one in which the English aristocracy was half French and contact between the two countries was close.

Romantic love, so important a theme in Western literature, apparently originated with the stories of courtly love composed by the troubadours of southern France in the late 11th and early 12th centuries. Courtly love has been described as the feudalization of erotic emotions and behavior in which the lover becomes the vassal of his lady. To the pages, squires, and knights, who constituted the court of the feudal baron, the lady of the castle with her ladies in waiting represented the feminine and gentle side of life. Few of these young men were in a position to marry; instead, they aspired to an illicit relationship with an almost unattainable and highly idealized mistress.

According to C. S. Lewis, courtly love involved "Humility, Courtesy, Adultery and the Religion of Love." These characteristics can be explained by the environment of the feudal court. Humility and courtesy were the hallmarks of devotion, and adultery was unavoidable because "any idealization of sexual love in a society where marriage was purely utilitarian must begin with an idealization of adultery." [12] The worship of love, as a goddess, was natural in a religious age in which the official church not only proscribed extramarital sex but often condemned passionate love itself as sinful—even within marriage.

Denis de Rougemont, another modern writer, believes that the idealization of eroticism by the cult of courtly love has distorted Western concepts of marriage ever since. For de Rougemont the lasting basis for marriage lies not in the self-centered (and destructive) passion which the Greeks called *eros,* but only in the sense of commitment and unselfish love which they and the writers of the New Testament described as *agape.*[13]

Lewis and de Rougemont undoubtedly exaggerate the significance of courtly love. Indeed, some recent writers suggest that courtly love is largely the invention of literary historians; certainly it seems questionable to speak of a "cult of courtly love."[14] On the other hand, the popularity of the romances of the troubadours and trouvères among the French and English aristocracy in the 12th and 13th centuries is beyond dispute. The relative decrease of warfare and the increase in the amenities of life produced a society which placed greater value on courteous behavior. It would also seem true that in this new environment youth, especially, revolted against a system which completely subordinated marriage to political and economic considerations. The concept of romantic love offered at least a literary escape from the sordid realities of castle and camp life.

The Lay of Milon

He who would tell divers tales must know how to vary the tune. To win the favour of any, he must speak to the understanding of all. I purpose in this place to show you the story of Milon, and—since few words are best—I will set out the adventure as briefly as I may.

Milon was born in South Wales. So great was his prowess that from the day he was dubbed knight there was no champion who could stand before him in the lists. He was a passing fair knight, open and brave, courteous to his friends, and stern to his foes. Men praised his name in whatever realm they talked of gallant deeds—Ireland, Norway, and Wales, yea, from Jutland even to Albania. Since he was praised by the frank, he was therefore envied of the mean. Nevertheless, by reason of his skill with the spear, he was counted a very worshipful knight, and was honourably entreated by many a prince in divers lands.

In Milon's own realm there lived a lord whose name has gone from mind. With this baron dwelt his daughter, a passing fair and gracious damsel. Much talk had this maiden heard of Milon's knightly deeds, so that she began to set her thoughts upon him, because of the good men spoke of him. She sent him a message by a sure hand, saying that if her love was to his mind, sweetly would it be to her heart. Milon rejoiced greatly when he knew this thing. He thanked the lady for her words, giving her love again in return for her own, and swearing that he would never depart therefrom any day of his days. Beyond this courteous answer Milon bestowed on the messenger costly gifts, and made him promises that were richer still.

"Friend," said he, "of your charity I pray you that I may have speech with my friend, in such a fashion that none shall know of our meeting. Carry her this, my golden ring. Tell her, on my part, that so she pleases she shall come to me, or, if it be her better pleasure, I will go to her."

The messenger bade farewell, and returned to his lady. He placed the ring in her hand, saying that he had done her will, as he was bidden to do.

Right joyous was the damsel to know that Milon's love was tender as her own. She required her friend to come for speech within the private garden of her house, where she was wont to take her delight. Milon came at her commandment. He came so often, and so dearly she loved him, that in the end she gave him all that maid may give. When the damsel perceived how it was with her, she sent messages to her friend, telling him of her case, and making great sorrow.

"I have lost my father and all his wealth," said the lady, "for when he hears of this matter he will make of me an example. Either I shall be tormented with the sword, or else he will sell me as a slave in a far country."

(For such was the usage of our fathers in the days of this tale.)

Milon grieved sorely, and made answer that he would do the thing the damsel thought most seemly to be done.

"When the child is born," replied the lady, "you must carry him forthwith to my sister. She is a rich dame, pitiful and good, and is wedded to a lord of Northumberland. You will send messages with the babe—both in writing and by speech—that the little innocent is her sister's child. Whether it be a boy or girl his mother will have suffered much because of him, and for her sister's sake you will pray her to cherish the babe. Beyond this I shall set your signet by a lace about his neck, and write letters wherein shall be made plain the name of his sire, and the sad story of his mother. When he shall have grown tall, and of an age to understand these matters, his aunt will give him your ring, and rehearse to him the letter. If this be done, perchance the orphan will not be fatherless all his days."

Milon approved the counsel of the lady, and when her time had come she was brought to bed of a boy. The old nurse who tended her mistress was privy to the damsel's inmost mind. So warily she went to work, so cunning was she in gloss and concealment, that none within the palace knew that there was aught to hide. The damsel looked upon her boy, and saw that he was very fair. She laced the ring about his neck, and set the letter that it were death to find, within a silken chatelaine. The child was then placed in his cradle, swathed close in white linen. A pillow of feathers was put beneath his head, and over all was laid a warm coverlet, wadded with fur. In this fashion the ancient nurse gave the babe to his father, who awaited him within the garden. Milon commended the child to his men, charging them to carry him loyally, by such towns as they knew, to that lady beyond the Humber. The servitors set forth, bearing the infant with them. Seven times a day they reposed them in their journey, so that the women might nourish the babe, and bathe and tend him duly. They served their lord so faithfully, keeping such watch upon the way, that at the last they won to the lady to whom they were bidden. The lady received them courteously, as became her breeding. She broke the seal of the letter, and when she was assured of what was therein, marvellously she cherished the infant. These having bestowed the boy in accordance with their lord's commandment, returned to their own land.

Milon went forth from his realm to serve beyond the seas for guerdon. His friend remained within her house and was granted by her father in marriage to a right rich baron of that country. Though this baron was a worthy knight, justly esteemed of all his fellows, the damsel was grieved beyond measure when she knew her father's will. She called to mind the past, and regretted that Milon had gone from the country, since he would have helped her in her need.

"Alas!" said the lady, "what shall I do? I doubt that I am lost, for my lord will find that his bride is not a maid. If this becomes known they will make me a bondwoman for all my days. Would that my friend were here to free me from this coil. It were good for me to die rather than to live, but by no means can I escape from their hands. They have set warders about me, men, old and young, whom they call my chamberlains, contemners of love, who delight themselves in sadness. But endure it I must, for, alas, I know not how to die."

So on the appointed day the lady was wedded to the baron, and her husband took her to dwell with him in his fief.

When Milon returned to his own country he was right heavy and sorrowful to learn of this marriage. He lamented his wretched case, but in this he found comfort, that he was not far from the realm where the lady abode whom so tenderly he loved. Milon commenced to think within himself how best he might send letters to the damsel that he was come again to his home, yet so that none should have knowledge thereof. He wrote a letter, and sealed it with his seal. This message he made fast to the neck, and hid within the plumage of a swan that was long his, and was greatly to his heart. He bade his squire to come, and made him his messenger.

"Change thy raiment swiftly," said he, "and hasten to the castle of my friend. Take with thee my swan, and see that none, neither servant nor handmaid, delivers the bird to my lady, save thyself alone."

The squire did according to his lord's commandment. He made him ready quickly, and went forth, bearing the swan with him. He went by the nearest road, and passing through the streets of the city, came before the portal of the castle. In answer to his summons the porter drew near.

"Friend," said he, "hearken to me. I am of Caerleon, and a fowler by craft. Within my nets I have snared the most marvellous swan in the world. This wondrous bird I would bestow forthwith upon your lady, but perforce I must offer her the gift with my own hand."

"Friend," replied the porter, "fowlers are not always welcomed of ladies. If you come with me I will bring you where I may know whether it pleases my lady to have speech with you and to receive your gift."

The porter entered in the hall, where he found none but two lords seated at a great table, playing chess for their delight. He swiftly returned on his steps, and the fowler with him, so furtively withal that the lords were not disturbed at their game, nor perceived aught of the matter. They went therefore to the chamber of the lady. In answer to their call the door was opened to them by a maiden, who led them before her dame. When the swan was proffered to the lady it pleased her to receive the gift. She summoned a varlet of her household and gave the bird to his charge, commanding him to keep it safely, and to see that it ate enough and to spare.

"Lady," said the servitor, "I will do your bidding. We shall never receive from any fowler on earth such another bird as this.

The swan is fit to serve at a royal table, for the bird is plump as he is fair."

The varlet put the swan in his lady's hands. She took the bird kindly, and smoothing his head and neck, felt the letter that was hidden beneath its feathers. The blood pricked in her veins, for well she knew that the writing was sent her by her friend. She caused the fowler to be given of her bounty, and bade the men to go forth from her chamber. When they had parted the lady called a maiden to her aid. She broke the seal, and unfastening the letter, came upon the name of Milon at the head. She kissed the name a hundred times through her tears. When she might read the writing she learned of the great pain and dolour that her lover suffered by day and by night. In you—he wrote—is all my pleasure, and in your white hands it lies to heal me or to slay. Strive to find a plan by which we may speak as friend to friend, if you would have me live. The knight prayed her in his letter to send him an answer by means of the swan. If the bird were well guarded, and kept without provand for three days, he would of a surety fly back to the place from whence he came, with any message that the lady might lace about his neck.

When the damsel had considered the writing, and understood what was put therein, she commanded that her bird should be tended carefully, and given plenteously to eat and to drink. She held him for a month within her chamber, but this was less from choice, than for the craft that was necessary to obtain the ink and parchment requisite for her writing. At the end she wrote a letter according to her heart, and sealed it with her ring. The lady caused the swan to fast for three full days; then having concealed the message about his neck, let him take his flight. The bird was all anhungered for food, and remembering well the home from which he drew, he returned thither as quickly as his wings might bear him.

He knew again his town, and his master's house, and descended to the ground at Milon's very feet. Milon rejoiced greatly when he marked his own. He caught the bird by his wings, and crying for his steward, bade him give the swan to eat. The knight removed the missive from the messenger's neck. He glanced from head to head of the letter, seeking the means that he hoped to find, and the salutation he so tenderly wished. Sweet to his heart was the writing, for the lady wrote that without him there was no joy in her life, and since it was his desire to hear by the swan, it would be her pleasure also.

For twenty years the swan was made the messenger of these two lovers, who might never win together. There was no speech between them, save that carried by the bird. They caused the swan to fast for three days, and then sent him on his errand. He to whom the letter came, saw to it that the messenger was fed to heart's desire. Many a time the swan went upon his journey, for however strictly the lady was held of her husband, there was none who had suspicion of a bird.

The dame beyond the Humber nourished and tended the boy committed to her charge with the greatest care. When he was come to a fitting age she made him to be knighted of her lord, for goodly and serviceable was the lad. On the same day the aunt read over to him the letter, and put in his hand the ring. She told him the name of his mother, and his father's story. In all the world there was no worthier knight, nor a more chivalrous and gallant gentleman. The lad hearkened diligently to the lady's tale. He rejoiced greatly to hear of his father's prowess, and was proud beyond measure of his renown. He considered within himself, saying to his own heart, that much should be required of his father's son, and that he would not be worthy of his blood if he did not endeavour to merit his name. He determined therefore that he would leave his country, and seek adventure as a knight errant, beyond the sea. The varlet delayed no longer than the evening. On the morrow he bade farewell to his aunt, who having warned and admonished him for his good, gave him largely of her wealth, to bring him on his way. He rode to Southampton, that he might find a ship equipped for sea, and so came to Barfleur. Without any tarrying the lad went straight to Brittany, where he spent his money and himself in feasts and in tourneys. The rich men of the land were glad of his friendship, for there was none who bore himself better in the press with spear or with sword. What he took from the rich he bestowed on such knights as were poor and luckless. These loved him greatly, since he gained largely and spent freely, granting of his wealth to all. Wherever this knight sojourned in the realm he bore away the prize. So debonair was he and chivalrous that his fame and praise crossed the water, and were noised abroad in his own land. Folk told how a certain knight from beyond the Humber, who had passed the sea in quest of wealth and honour, had so done, that by reason of his prowess, his liberality, and his modesty, men called him the Knight Peerless, since they did not know his name.

This praise of the good knight, and of his deeds, came to be heard of Milon. Very dolent was he and sorely troubled that so young a knight should be esteemed above his fathers. He marvelled greatly that the stout spears of the past had not put on their harness and broken a lance for their ancient honour. One thing he determined, that he would cross the sea without delay, so that he might joust with the dansellon, and abate his pride. In wrath and anger he purposed to fight, to beat his adversary from the saddle, and bring him at last to shame. After this was ended he would seek his son, of whom he had heard nothing, since he had gone from his aunt's castle. Milon caused his friend to know of his wishes. He opened out to her all his thought, and craved her permission to depart. This letter he sent by the swan, commending the bird to her care.

When the lady heard of her lover's purpose, she thanked him for his courtesy, for greatly was his counsel to her mind. She approved his desire to quit the realm for the sake of his honour, and far from putting let and hindrance in his path, trusted that in the end he would bring again her son. Since Milon was assured of his friend's goodwill, he arrayed himself richly, and crossing the sea to Normandy, came afterwards into the land of the Bretons. There he sought the friendship of the lords of that realm, and fared to all the tournaments of which he might hear. Milon bore himself proudly, and gave graciously of his wealth, as though he were receiving a gift. He sojourned till the winter was past in that land, he, and a brave company of knights whom he held in his house with him. When Easter had come, and the season that men give to tourneys and wars and the righting of their private wrongs, Milon considered how he could meet with the knight whom men called Peerless. At that time a tournament was proclaimed to be held at Mont St. Michel. Many a Norman and Breton rode to the game; knights of Flanders and of France were there in plenty, but few fared from England. Milon drew to the lists amongst the first. He inquired diligently of the young champion, and all men were ready to tell from whence he came, and of his harness, and of the blazon on his shield. At length the knight appeared in the lists and Milon looked upon the adversary he so greatly desired to see. Now in this tournament a knight could joust with that lord who was set over against him, or he could seek to break a lance with his chosen foe. A player must gain or lose, and he might find himself opposed either by his comrade or his enemy. Milon did well and worshipfully in the press, and was praised of many that day. But the Knight Peerless carried the cry from all his fellows, for none might stand before him, nor rival him in skill and address. Milon observed him curiously. The lad struck so heavily, he thrust home so shrewdly, that Milon's hatred changed to envy as he watched. Very comely showed the varlet, and much to Milon's mind. The older knight set himself over against the champion, and they met together in the centre of the field. Milon struck his adversary so fiercely, that the lance splintered in his gauntlet; but the young knight kept his seat without even losing a stirrup. In return his spear was aimed with such cunning that he bore his antagonist to the ground. Milon lay upon the earth bareheaded, for his helmet was unlaced in the shock. His hair and beard showed white to all, and the varlet was heavy to look on him whom he had overthrown. He caught the destrier by the bridle, and led him before the stricken man.

"Sir," said he, "I pray you to get upon your horse. I am right grieved and vexed that I should have done this wrong. Believe me that it was wrought unwittingly."

Milon sprang upon his steed. He approved the courtesy of his adversary, and looking upon the hand that held his bridle, he knew again his ring. He made inquiry of the lad.

"Friend," said he, "hearken to me. Tell me now the name of thy sire. How art thou called; who is thy mother? I have seen much, and gone to and fro about the world. All my life I have journeyed from realm to realm, by reason of tourneys and quarrels and princes' wars, yet never once by any knight have I been borne from my horse. This day I am overthrown by a boy, and yet I cannot help but love thee."

The varlet answered,

"I know little of my father. I understand that his name is Milon, and that he was a knight of Wales. He loved the daughter of a rich man, and was loved again. My mother bore me in secret, and caused me to be carried to Northumberland, where I was taught and tended. An old aunt was at the costs of my nourishing. She kept me at her side, till of all her gifts she gave me horse and arms, and sent me here, where I have remained. In hope and wish I purpose to cross the sea, and return to my own realm. There I would seek out my father, and learn how it stands between him and my mother. I will show him my golden ring, and I will tell him of such privy matters that he may not deny our kinship, but must love me as a son, and ever hold me dear."

When Milon heard these words he could endure them no further. He got him swiftly from his horse, and taking the lad by the fringe of his hauberk, he cried,

"Praise be to God, for now am I healed. Fair friend, by my faith thou art my very son, for whom I came forth from my own land, and have sought through all this realm."

The varlet climbed from the saddle, and stood upon his feet. Father and son kissed each other tenderly, with many comfortable words. Their love was fair to see, and those who looked upon their meeting, wept for joy and pity.

Milon and his son departed from the tournament so soon as it came to an end, for the knight desired greatly to speak to the varlet at leisure, and to open before him all his mind. They rode to their hostel, and with the knights of their fellowship, passed the hours in mirth and revelry. Milon spoke to the lad of his mother. He told him of their long love, and how she was given by her father in marriage to a baron of his realm. He rehearsed the years of separation, accepted by both with a good heart, and of the messenger who carried letters between them, when there was none they dared to trust in, save only the swan.

The son made answer,

"In faith, fair father, let us return to our own land. There I will slay this husband, and you shall yet be my mother's lord."

This being accorded between them, on the morrow they made them ready for the journey, and bidding farewell to their friends, set forth for Wales. They embarked in a propitious hour, for a fair wind carried the ship right swiftly to its haven. They had not ridden far upon their road, when they met a certain squire of the lady's household on his way to Brittany, bearing letters to Milon. His task was done long before sundown in chancing on the knight. He gave over the sealed writing with which he was charged, praying the knight to hasten to his friend without any tarrying, since her husband was in his grave. Milon rejoiced greatly when he knew this thing. He showed the message to his son, and pressed forward without pause or rest. They made such speed, that at the end they came to the castle where the lady had her lodging. Light of heart was she when she clasped again her child. These two fond lovers sought neither countenance of their kin, nor counsel of any man. Their son handselled them together, and gave the mother to his sire. From the day they were wed they dwelt in wealth and in sweetness to the end of their lives.

Of their love and content the minstrel wrought this Lay. I, also, who have set it down in writing, have won guerdon enough just by telling over the tale.

The Chatelaine of Vergi

There are divers men who make a great show of loyalty, and pretend to such discretion in the hidden things they hear, that at the end folk come to put faith in them. When by their false seeming they have persuaded the simple to open out to them their love and their deeds, then they noise the matter about the country, and make it their song and their mirth. Thus it chances that the lesser joy is his who has bared to them his heart. For the sweeter the love, the more bitter is the pang that lovers know, when each deems the other to have bruited abroad the secret he should conceal. Oftentimes these blabbers do such mischief with their tongue, that the love they spoil comes to its close in sorrow and in care. This indeed happened in Burgundy to a brave and worthy knight, and to the Lady of Vergi. This knight loved his lady so dearly that she granted him her tenderness, on such covenant as this—that the day he showed her favour to any, that very hour he would lose the love and the grace she bestowed on him. To seal this bond they devised together that the knight should come a days to an orchard, at such hour as seemed good to his friend. He must remain coy in his nook within the wall till he might see the lady's lapdog run across the orchard. Then without further tarrying he should enter her chamber, knowing full well she was alone, whom so fondly he desired to greet. This he did, and in this fashion they met together for a great while, none being privy to their sweet and stolen love, save themselves alone.

The knight was courteous and fair, and by reason of his courage was right welcome to that Duke who was lord of Burgundy. He came and went about the Court, and that so often that the Duchess set her mind upon him. She cared so little to hide her thought, that had his heart not been in another's keeping, he must surely have perceived in her eyes that she loved him. But however tender her semblance the knight showed no kindness in return, for he marked nothing of her inclination. Passing troubled was the dame that he should treat her thus; so that on a day she took him apart, and sought to make him of her counsel.

"Sir, as men report, you are a brave and worthy knight, for the which give God thanks. It would not be more than your deserts, if you had for friend a lady in so high a place that her love would bring to you both honour and profit. How richly could such a lady serve you!"

"Lady," said he, "I have never yet had this in my thought."

"By my faith," she answered, "it seems to me that the longer you wait, the less is your hope. Perchance the lady will stoop very readily from her throne, if you but kneel at her knee."

The knight replied,

"Lady, by my faith, I know little why you speak such words, and I understand their meaning not at all. I am neither duke nor count to dare to set my love in so high a seat. There is nought in me to gain the love of so sovereign a dame, pain me how I may."

"Such things have been," said she, "and so may chance again. Many more marvellous works have been wrought than this, and the day of miracles is not yet past. Tell me, know you not yet that you have gained the love of some high princess, even mine?"

The knight made answer forthwith,

"Lady, I know it not. I would desire to have your love in a fair and honourable fashion; but may God keep me from such love between us, as would put shame upon my lord. In no manner, nor for any reason, will I enter on such a business as would lead me to deal my true and lawful lord so shrewd and foul a wrong."

Bitter at heart was the dame to see her love so scorned.

"Fie upon you," she cried, "and who required of you any such thing?"

"Ah, lady, to God be the praise; you have said enough to make your meaning passing plain."

The lady strove no more to show herself kind to him. Great was the wrath and sharp the malice that she hid within her heart, and well she purposed that, if she might, she would avenge herself speedily. All the day she considered her anger. That night as she lay beside the Duke she began to sigh, and afterwards to weep. Presently the Duke inquired of her grief, bidding her show it him forthwith.

"Certes," said the dame, "I make this great sorrow because no prince can tell who is his faithful servant, and who is not. Often he gives the more honour and wealth to those who are traitors rather than friends, and sees nothing of their wrong."

"In faith, wife," answered the Duke, "I know not why you speak these words. At least I am free of such blame as this, for in nowise would I nourish a traitor, if only a traitor I knew him to be."

"Hate then this traitor," cried she—and she named a name—"who gives me no peace, praying and requiring me the livelong day that I should grant him my love. For a great while he had been in this mind—as he says—but did not dare to speak his thoughts. I considered the whole matter, fair lord, and resolved to show it you at once. It is likely enough to be true that he cherished this hope, for we have never heard that he loves elsewhere. I entreat you in guerdon, to look well to your own honour, since this, as you know, is your duty and right."

Passing grievous was this business to the Duke. He answered to the lady,

"I will bring it to a head, and very quickly, as I deem."

That night the Duke lay upon a bed of little ease. He could neither sleep nor rest, by reason of that lord, his friend, who, he was persuaded, had done him such bitter wrong as justly to have forfeited his love. Because of this he kept vigil the whole night through. He rose very early on the morrow, and bade him come whom his wife had put to blame, although he had done nothing blameworthy. Then he took him to task, man to man, when there were but these two together.

"Certes," he said, "it is a heavy grief that you who are so comely and brave, should yet have no honour in you. You have deceived me the more, for I have long believed you to be a man of good faith, giving loyalty, at least, to me, in return for the love I have given to you. I know not how you can have harboured such a felon's wish, as to pray and require the Duchess to grant you her grace. You are guilty of such treachery that conduct more vile it would be far to seek. Get you hence from my realm. You have my leave to part, and it is denied to you for ever. If you return here it will be at your utmost peril, for I warn you beforehand that if I lay hands upon you, you will die a shameful death."

When the knight heard this judgment, such wrath and mortification were his that his members trembled beneath him. He called to mind his friend, of whom he would have no joy, if he might not come and go and sojourn in that realm from which the Duke had banished him. Moreover he was sick at heart that his lord should deem him a disloyal traitor, without just cause. He knew such sore discomfort that he held himself as dead and betrayed.

"Sire," said he, "for the love of God believe this never, neither think that I have been so bold. To do that of which you wrongfully charge me, has never entered my mind, not one day, nor for one single hour. Who has told you this lie has wrought a great ill."

"You gain nothing by such denials," answered the Duke, "for of a surety the thing is true. I have heard from her own lips the very guise and fashion in which you prayed and required her love, like the envious traitor that you are. Many another word it may well be that you spoke, as to which the lady of her courtesy keeps silence."

"My lady says what it pleases her to say," replied the dolorous knight, "and my denials are lighter than her word. Naught is there for me to say; nothing is left for me to do, so that I may be believed that this adventure never happened."

"Happen it did, by my soul," said the Duke, remembering certain words of his wife. Well he deemed that he might be assured of the truth, if but the lady's testimony were true that this lord had never loved otherwhere. Therefore the Duke said to the knight,

"If you will pledge your faith to answer truly what I may ask, I shall be certified by your words whether or not you have done this deed of which I misdoubt you."

The knight had but one desire—to turn aside his lord's wrath, which had so wrongfully fallen upon him. He feared only lest he should be driven from the land where lodged the dame who was the closest to his mind. Knowing nothing of what was in the Duke's thought, he considered that his question could only concern the one matter; so he replied that without fraud or concealment he would do as his lord had said. Thus he pledged his faith, and the Duke accepted his affiance.

When this was done the Duke made question,

"I have loved you so dearly that at the bottom of my heart I cannot believe you guilty of such shameless misdoing as the Duchess tells me. I would not credit it a moment, if you yourself were not the cause of my doubtfulness. From your face, the care you bestow upon your person, and a score of trifles, any who would know, can readily see that you are in love with some lady. Since none about the Court perceives damsel or dame on whom you have set your heart, I ask myself whether indeed it may not be my wife, who tells me that you have entreated her for love. Nothing that any one may do can take this suspicion from my mind, except you tell me yourself that you love elsewhere, making it so plain that I am left without doubt that I know the naked truth. If you refuse her name you will have broken your oath, and forth from my realm you go as an outlawed man."

The knight had none to give him counsel. To himself he seemed to stand at the parting of two ways, both one and the other leading to death. If he spoke the simple truth (and tell he must if he would not be a perjurer) then was he as good as dead; for if he did such wrong as to sin against the covenant with his lady and his friend, certainly he would lose her love, so it came to her knowledge. But if he concealed the truth from the Duke, then he was false to his oath, and had lost both country and friend. But little he recked of country, so only he might keep his Love, since of all his riches she was the most dear. The knight called to heart and remembrance the fair joy and the solace that were his when he had this lady between his arms. He considered within himself that if by reason of his misdoing she came to harm, or were lost to him, since he might not take her where he went, how could he live without her. It would be with him also, as erst with the Castellan of Couci, who having his Love fast only in his heart, told over in his song,

> Ah, God, strong Love, I sit and weep alone,
>   Remembering the solace that was given;
> The tender guise, the semblance* that was shown
>   By her, my friend, my comrade, and my Heaven.
>
> When grief brings back the joy that was mine own,
>   I would the heart from out my breast were riven.
> Ah, Lord, the sweet words hushed, the beauty flown;
>   Would God that I were dead, and low, and shriven.

The knight was in anguish such as this, for he knew not whether to make clear the truth, or to lie and be banished from the country.

Whilst he was deep in thought, turning over in his mind what it were best to do, tears rose in his heart and flowed from his eyes, so that his face was wet, by reason of the sorrow that he suffered. The Duke had no more mirth than the knight, deeming that his secret was so heavy that he dared not make it plain. The Duke spoke swiftly to his friend,

"I see clearly that you fear to trust me wholly, as a knight should trust his lord. If you confess your counsel privily to me, you cannot think that I shall show the matter to any man. I would rather have my teeth drawn one by one, than speak a word."

"Ah," cried the knight, "for God's love, have pity, Sire. I know not what I ought to say, nor what will become of me; but I would rather die than lose what lose I shall if she only hears that you have the truth, and that you heard it from my lips, whilst I am a living man."

The Duke made answer,

"I swear to you by my body and my soul, and on the faith and love I owe you again by reason of your homage, that never in my life will I tell the tale to any creature born, or even breathe a word or make a sign about the business."

With the tears yet running down his face the knight said to him,

"Sire, right or wrong, now will I show my secret. I love your niece of Vergi, and she loves me, so that no friends can love more fondly."

"If you wish to be believed," replied the Duke, "tell me now, if any, save you two alone, knows anything of this joy?"

And the knight made answer to him,

"Nay, not a creature in the world."

Then said the Duke,

"No love is so privy as that. If none has heard thereof, how do you meet together, and how devise time and place?"

"By my faith, Sire, I will tell you all, and keep back nothing, since you know so much of our counsel."

So he related the whole story of his goings to and fro within the pleasaunce; of that first covenant with his friend, and of the office of the little dog.

Then said the Duke,

"I require of you that I may be your comrade at such fair meeting. When you go again to the orchard, I too, would enter therein, and mark for myself the success of your device. As for my niece she shall perceive naught."

"Sire, if it be your will it is my pleasure also; save, only, that you find it not heavy or burdensome. Know well that I go this very night."

The Duke said that he would go with him, for the vigil would in no wise be burdensome, but rather a frolic and a game. They accorded between them a place of meeting, where they would draw together on foot, and alone. When nightfall was come they fared to the hostel of the Duke's niece, for her dwelling was near at hand. They had not tarried long in the garden, when the Duke saw his niece's lapdog run straight to that end of the orchard where the knight was hidden. Wondrous kindness showed the knight to his lady's dog. Immediately he took his way to her lodging, and left his master in his nook by the wall. The Duke followed after till he drew near the chamber, and held himself coy, concealing him as best he might. It was easy enough to do this, for a great tree stood there, high and leafy, so that he was covered close as by a shield. From this place he marked the little dog enter the chamber, and presently saw his niece issue therefrom, and hurry forth to meet her lover in the pleasaunce. He was so close that he could see and hear the solace of that greeting, the salutation of her mouth and of her hands. She embraced him closely in her fair white arms, kissing him more than a hundred times, whilst she spoke many comforting words. The knight for his part kissed her again, and held her fast, praising her with many tender names.

"My lady, my friend, my love," said he, "heart and mistress and hope, and the sum of all that I hold dear, know well that I have yearned to be with you as we are now, every day and all day long since we met."

"Sweet lord, sweet friend, sweet love," replied the lady, "never has a day nor an hour gone by but I was awearied of its length. But I grieve no longer over the past, for I have my heart's desire when you are with me, joyous and well. Right welcome are you to your friend."

And the knight made answer,

"Love, you are welcome and wellmet."

From his place of hiding, near the entrance to the chamber, the Duke hearkened to every word. His niece's voice and face were so familiar to him, that he could not doubt that the Duchess had lied. Greatly was he content, for he was now assured that his friend had not done amiss in that of which he had misdoubted him. All through the night he kept watch and ward. But during his vigil the dame and the knight, close and sleepless in the chamber, knew such joy and tenderness as it is not seemly should be told or heard, save of those who hope themselves to attain such solace, when Love grants them recompense for all their pains. For he who desires nothing of this joy and quittance, even if it were told him, would but listen to a tongue he could not understand, since his heart is not turned to Love, and none can know the wealth of such riches, except Love whisper it in his ear. Of such kingdom not all are worthy: for there joy goes without anger, and solace is crowned with fruition. But so fleet are things sweet, that to the lover his joy seems to find but a brief content. So pleasant is the life he passes that he wishes his night a week, his week to stretch to a month, the month become a year, and one year three, and three years twenty, and the twenty attain to a hundred. Yea, when the term and end were reached, he would that the dusk were closing, rather than the dawn had come.

This was the case with the lover whom the Duke awaited in the orchard. When day was breaking, and he durst remain no longer, he came with his lady to the door. The Duke marked the fashion of their leave-taking, the kisses given and granted, the sighs and the weeping as they bade farewell. When they had wept many tears, and devised an hour for their next meeting, the knight departed in this fashion, and the lady shut the door. But so long as she might see him, she followed his going with her pretty eyes, since there was nothing better she could do.

When the Duke knew the postern was made fast, he hastened on his road until he overtook the knight, who to himself was making his complaint of the season, that all too short was his hour. The same thought and the self same words were hers from whom he had parted, for the briefness of the time had betrayed her delight, and she had no praises for the dawn. The knight was deep in his thought and speech, when he was overtaken by the Duke. The Duke embraced his friend, greeting him very tenderly. Then he said to him,

"I pledge my faith that I will love you all the days of my life, never on any day seeking to do you a mischief, for you have told me the very truth, and have not lied to me by a single word."

"Sire," he made answer, "thanks and gramercy. But for the love of God I require and pray of you that it be your pleasure to hide this counsel; for I should lose my love, and the peace and comfort of my life—yea, and should die without sin of my own, if I deemed that any other in this realm than yourself knew aught of the business."

"Now speak of it never," replied the Duke. "Know that the counsel shall be kept so hidden, that by me shall not a syllable be spoken."

On this covenant they came again whence they had set forth together. That day, when men sat at meat, the Duke showed to his knight a friendlier semblance and a fairer courtesy than ever he had done before. The Duchess felt such wrath and despitefulness at this, that—without any leasing—she rose from the table, and making pretence of sudden sickness, went to lie upon her bed, where she found little softness. When the Duke had eaten and washed and made merry, he afterwards sought his wife's chamber, and causing her to be seated on her bed, commanded that none should remain, save himself. So all men went forth at his word, even as he had bidden. Thereupon the Duke inquired of the lady how this evil had come to her, and of what she was sick. She made answer,

"As God hears me, never till I ate at table did I deem that you had so little sense or decency, as when I saw you making much of him, who, I have told you already, strove to bring shame and disgrace on me. When I watched you entreat him with more favour than even was your wont, such great sorrow and such great anger took hold on me, that I could not contain myself in the hall."

"Sweet friend," replied the Duke, "know that I shall never believe—either from your lips or from those of any creature in the world—that the story ever happened as you rehearsed it. I am so deep in his counsel that he has my quittance, for I have full assurance that he never dreamed of such a deed. But as to this you must ask of me no more."

The Duke went straightway from the chamber, leaving the lady sunk in thought. However long she had to live, never might she know an hour's comfort, till she had learnt something of that secret of which the Duke forbade her to seek further. No denial could now stand in her way, for in her heart swiftly she devised a means to unriddle this counsel, so only she might endure until the evening, and the Duke was in her arms. She was persuaded that, beyond doubt, such solace would win her wish more surely than wrath or tears. For this purpose she held herself coy, and when the Duke came to lie at her side she betook herself to the further side of the bed, making semblance that his company gave her no pleasure. Well she knew that such show of anger was the device to put her lord beneath her feet. Therefore she turned her back upon him, that the Duke might the more easily be drawn by the cords of her wrath. For this same reason when he had no more than kissed her, she burst out,

"Right false and treacherous and disloyal are you to make such a pretence of affection, who yet have never loved me truly one single day. All these years of our wedded life I have been foolish enough to believe, what you took such pains in the telling, that you loved me with a loyal heart. To-day I see plainly that I was the more deceived."

"In what are you deceived?" inquired the Duke.

"By my faith," cried she, who was sick of her desire, "you warn me that I be not so bold as to ask aught of that of which you know the secret."

"In God's name, sweet wife, of what would you know?"

"Of all that he has told you, the lies and the follies he has put in your mind, and led you to believe. But it matters little now whether I hear it or not, for I remember how small is my gain in being your true and loving wife. For good or for ill I have shown you all my counsel. There was nothing that was known and seen of my heart that you were not told at once; and of your courtesy you repay me by concealing your mind. Know, now, without doubt, that never again shall I have in you such affiance, nor grant you my love with such sweetness, as I have bestowed them in the past."

Thereat the Duchess began to weep and sigh, making the most tender sorrow that she was able. The Duke felt such pity for her grief that he said to her,

"Fairest and dearest, your wrath and anger are more heavy than I can bear; but learn that I cannot tell what you wish me to say without sinning against my honour too grievously."

Then she replied forthwith,

"Husband, if you do not tell me, the reason can only be that you do not trust me to keep silence in the business. I wonder the more sorely at this, because there is no matter, either great or small, that you have told me, which has been published by me. I tell you honestly that never in my life could I be so indiscreet."

When she had said this, she betook her again to her tears. The Duke kissed and embraced her, and was so sick of heart that strength failed him to keep his purpose.

"Fair wife," he said to her, "by my soul I am at my wits' end. I have such trust and faith in you that I deem I should hide nothing, but show you all that I know. Yet I dread that you will let fall some word. Know, wife—and I tell it you again—that if ever you betray this counsel you will get death for your payment."

The Duchess made answer,

"I agree to the bargain, for it is not possible that I should deal you so shrewd a wrong."

Then he who loved her, because of his faith and his credence in her word, told all this story of his niece, even as he had learned it from the knight. He told how those two were alone together in the shadow of the wall, when the little dog ran to them. He showed plainly of that coming forth from the chamber, and of the entering in; nothing was hid, he concealed naught of that he had heard and seen. When the Duchess understood that the love of a mighty dame was despised for the sake of a lowly gentlewoman, her humiliation was bitter in her mouth as death. She showed no semblance of despitefulness, but made covenant and promise with the Duke to keep the matter close, saying that should she repeat his tale he might hang her from a tree.

Time went very heavily with the lady, till she could get speech with her, whom she hated from the hour she knew her to be the friend of him who had caused her such shame and grief. She was persuaded that for this reason he would not give her love, in return for that she set on him. She confirmed herself in her purpose, that at such time and place she saw the Duke speaking with his niece, she would go swiftly to the lady, and tell out all her mind, hiding nothing because it was evil. Neither time nor place was met, till Pentecost was come, and the Duke held high Court, commanding to the feast all the ladies of his realm, amongst the first that lady, his niece, who was the Chatelaine of Vergi. When the Duchess looked on her, the blood pricked in her veins, for reason that she hated her more than aught else in the world. She had the courage to hide her malice, and greeted the lady more gladly then ever she had done before. But she yearned to show openly the anger that burned in her heart, and the delay was much against her mind. On Pentecost, whilst the tables were removed, the Duchess brought the ladies to her chamber with her, that, apart from the throng, they might the more graciously attire them for the dance. She deemed her hour had come, and having no longer the power to refrain her lips, she said gaily, as if in jest,

"Chatelaine, array yourself very sweetly, since there is a fair and worthy lord you have to please."

The lady answered right simply,

"In truth, madam, I know not what you are thinking of; but for my part I wish for no such friendship as may not be altogether according to my honour and to that of my lord."

"I grant that readily," replied the Duchess, "you are a good mistress, and have an apt pupil in your little dog."

The ladies returned with the Duchess to the hall, where the dances were already set. They had listened to the tale, but could not mark the jest. The chatelaine remained in the chamber. Her colour came and went, and because of her wrath and trouble the heart throbbed thickly in her breast. She passed within a tiring chamber, where a little maiden was lying at the foot of the bed; but for grief she might not perceive her. The chatelaine flung herself upon the bed, bewailing her evil plight, for she was exceedingly sorrowful. She said,

"Ah, Lord God, take pity on me! What may this mean, that I have listened to my lady's reproaches because of the training of my little dog! This she can have learned from none—as well I know—save from him whom I have loved, and who has betrayed me. He would never have shown her this thing, except that he was her familiar friend, and doubtless loves her more dearly than me, whom he has betrayed. I see now the value of his oaths, since he finds it so easy to fail in his covenant. Sweet God, and I loved him so fondly, more fondly than any woman has loved before; who never had him from my thoughts one single hour, whether it were night or day. For he was my mirth and my carol; in him were my joy and my pleasure; he alone was my solace and comfort. Ah, my friend, how can this have come;

you who were always with me, even when I might not see you with my eyes! What ill has befallen you, that you durst prove false to me? I deemed you more faithful—God take me in His keeping—than ever was Tristan to Isolde. May God pity a poor fool, I loved you half as much again than I had love for myself. From the first to the last of our friendship, never by thought, or by word, or by deed, have I done amiss; there is no wrong doing, trifling or great, to make plain your hatred, or to excuse so vile a betrayal as this scorning of our love for a fresher face, this desertion of me, this proclaiming of our secret. Alas, my friend, I marvel greatly; for as God is my witness my heart was not thus towards you. If God had offered me all the kingdoms of the world, yea, and His Heaven and its Paradise besides, I would have refused them gladly, had my gain meant the losing of you. For you were my wealth and my song and my health, and nothing can hurt me any more, since my heart has learnt that yours no longer loves me. Ah, lasting, precious love! Who could have guessed that he would deal this blow, to whom I gave the grace of my tenderness—who said that I was his lady both in body and in soul, and he the slave at my bidding. Yea, he told it over so sweetly, that I believed him faithfully, nor thought in any wise that his heart would bear wrath and malice against me, whether for Duchess or for Queen. How good was this love, since the heart in my breast must always cleave to his! I counted him to be my friend, in age as in youth, our lives together; for well I knew that if he died first I should not dare to endure long without him, because of the greatness of my love. The grave, with him, would be fairer, than life in a world where I might never see him with my eyes. Ah, lasting, precious love! Is it then seemly that he should publish our counsel, and destroy her who had done him no wrong? When I gave him my love without grudging, I warned him plainly, and made covenant with him, that he would lose me the self same hour that he made our tenderness a song. Since part we must, I may not live after so bitter a sorrow; nor would I choose to live, even if I were able. Fie upon life, it has no savour in it. Since it pleases me naught, I pray to God to grant me death, and—so truly as I have loved him who requites me thus—to have mercy on my soul. I forgive him his wrong, and may God give honour and life to him who has betrayed and delivered me to death. Since it comes from his hand, death, meseems, is no bitter potion; and when I remember his love, to die for his sake is no grievous thing."

When the chatelaine had thus spoken she kept silence, save only that she said in sighing,

"Sweet friend, I commend you to God."

With these words she strained her arms tightly across her breast, the heart failed her, and her face lost its fair colour. She swooned in her anguish, and lay back, pale and discoloured in the middle of the bed, without life or breath.

Of this her friend knew nothing, for he sought his delight in the hall, at carol and dance and play. But amongst all those ladies he had no pleasure in any that he saw, since he might not perceive her to whom his heart was given, and much he marvelled thereat. He took the Duke apart, and said in his ear,

"Sire, whence is this that your niece tarries so long, and comes not to the dancing? Have you put her in prison?"

The Duke looked upon the dancers, for he had not concerned himself with the revels. He took his friend by the hand, and led him directly to his wife's chamber. When he might not find her there he bade the knight seek her boldly in the tiring chamber; and this he did of his courtesy that these two lovers might solace themselves with clasp and kiss. The knight thanked his lord sweetly, and entered softly in the chamber, where his friend lay dark and discoloured upon the bed. Time and place being met together, he took her in his arms and touched her lips. But when he found how cold was her mouth, how pale and rigid her person, he knew by the semblance of all her body that she was quite dead. In his amazement he cried out swiftly,

"What is this? Alas, is my dear one dead?"

The maiden started from the foot of the bed where she still lay, making answer,

"Sir, I deem truly that she be dead. Since she came to this room she has done nothing but call upon death, by reason of her friend's falsehood, whereof my lady assured her, and because of a little dog, whereof my lady made her jest. This sorrow brought her to her death."

When the knight understood from this that the words he had spoken to the Duke had slain his friend, he was discomforted beyond measure.

"Alas," said he, "sweet love, the most gracious and the best that ever knight had, loyal and true, how have I slain you, like the faithless traitor that I am! It were only just that I should receive the wages for my deed, so that you could have gone free of blame. But you were so faithful of heart that you took it on yourself to pay the price. Then I will do justice on myself for the treason I have wrought."

The knight drew from its sheath a sword that was hanging from the wall, and thrust it through his heart. He pained himself to fall upon his lady's body; and because of the mightiness of his hurt, bled swiftly to death. The maiden fled forth from the chamber, when she marked these lifeless lovers, for she was all adread at what she saw. She lighted on the Duke, and told him all that she had heard and seen, keeping back nothing. She showed him the beginning of the matter, and also of the little dog, whereof the Duchess had spoken.

Hearken all to what befell. The Duke went straightway to the tiring chamber, and drew from out the wound that sword by which the knight lay slain. He said no word, but hastened forthwith to the hall where the guests were yet at their dancing. Entering there he acquitted himself of his promise, for he smote the Duchess on the head with the naked sword he carried in his hand. He struck the blow without one word, since his wrath was too deep for speech. The Duchess fell at his feet, in the sight of the barons of his realm, whereat the feast was sorely troubled, for in place of mirth and carol, now were blood and death. Then the Duke told loudly and swiftly, before all who cared to hear, this pitiful story, in the midst of his Court. There was not one but wept, and his tears were the more piteous when he beheld those two lovers who lay dead in the chamber, and the Duchess in her hall. So the Court broke up in dole and anger, for of this deed came mighty mischief. On the morrow the Duke caused the lovers to be laid in one tomb, and the Duchess in a place apart. But of this adventure the Duke had such bitterness that never was he known to laugh again. He took the Cross, and went beyond the sea, where joining himself to the Knights Templar, he never returned to his own realm.

Ah, God! all this mischief and encumbrance chanced to the knight by reason of his making plain that he should have hid, and of publishing what his friend forbade him to speak, if he would keep her love. From this ensample we may learn that it is not seemly to love, and tell. He who blabs and blazons his friendship gets not one kiss the more; but he who goes discreetly preserves life and love and fame. For the friendship of the discreet lover falls not before the mine of such false and felon pryers as burrow privily into their neighbour's secret love.

NOTES TO CHAPTER III

1. Sidney Painter, *French Chivalry: Chivalric Ideas and Practices in Medieval France* (Johns Hopkins University Press, 1940; reprint ed., Ithaca, N.Y.: Cornell University Press, 1957), chap. 3.
2. K. R. Potter, ed. and trans., *The Deeds of Stephen* (London: Thomas Nelson and Sons, 1955), p. 93. Reprinted by permission of the publisher.
3. Ibid., p. 1.
4. Quoted in Frank Barlow, *The Feudal Kingdom of England, 1042-1216* (London: Longmans, Green, 1955), p. 252.
5. *Men in Groups* (New York: Random House, 1969), chap. 3.
6. *Griffon* is the medieval French word for *Greek*. William III and Tancred came from a French dynasty that had conquered Sicily, but Sicily had once been part of the Byzantine Empire and the anti-papal party there was apparently known as *Greeks* or *Griffons*.
7. Hugh the Brown was the son and heir of Count de la Marche, a French vassal of King Richard. Later in 1200, Richard's brother King John married

Isabelle of Angouleme, who had been betrothed to Hugh the Brown. Hugh then appealed to King Philip II of France for justice, and the ensuing dispute led to a war between John and Philip as a result of which John lost Normandy.

8. *The Reign of King John* (Baltimore: Johns Hopkins University Press, 1950), p. 238.

9. Bryce D. Lyon, *From Fief to Indenture: The Transition from Feudal to Non-Feudal Contract in Western Europe* (Cambridge, Mass.: Harvard University Press, 1957), pp. 201-7.

10. A. L. Poole, *From Domesday Book to Magna Carta, 1087-1216* (Oxford: Clarendon Press, 1955), pp. 476-77.

11. V. H. Galbraith, *Roger of Wendover and Mathew Paris* (Glasgow: Jackson and Son, 1944), pp. 15-20.

12. C. S. Lewis, *The Allegory of Love: A Study in Medieval Tradition* (New York: Oxford University Press, 1936; reprint ed., 1959), pp. 12, 13.

13. *Love in the Western World,* trans. Montgomery Belgion (New York: Harcourt Brace, 1956), chap. 7.

14. F. X. Newman, ed., *The Meaning of Courtly Love* (Albany: State University Press of New York, 1968). See especially the essay by John F. Benton, "Clio and Venus: An Historical View of Medieval Love," pp. 19-54.

CHAPTER IV
Popular Medieval Religion

DURING THE 12th and 13th centuries medieval theology achieved a high level of sophistication, particularly in the new universities. While intellectuals were forging scholastic philosophy, others were interpreting Christianity in terms meaningful to everyday experience. The religious spirit of the age found popular expression in literature and in art forms, such as the magnificent cathedrals that embodied the craftsmanship of thousands of artisans.

One of the strengths of the medieval church was that it fostered among people of all classes a sense of the love of God and his saints for ordinary men and women. Numerous tales of miracles related how the saints would protect men from danger and disaster, even from the consequences of their own sins. Among the saints, the Virgin came to be thought of as especially concerned with everyday life. Stories of her intercession humanized the formal creed of the church, which seemed to condemn so many to damnation.[1] Saint Bernard explained that although Christ might be man's mediator before God, most men were overawed by His majesty. "Flee to Mary," he wrote, "whose pure humanity the Son also honors. The Son hears the Mother, the Father the Son." [2]

In addition to the tales of miracles, other stories, such as *The Priest and the Mulberries* given below, illustrate how people found a religious meaning in ordinary occurrences. An even more important manifestation of popular religion appeared with the mystery and morality plays of the later Middle Ages. These dramatized the teachings of the church in a manner at the same time entertaining and didactic. An example of both types of play is included in this chapter.

Johannes Herolt's Miracles of the Blessed Virgin Mary
(12th to 15th Centuries)

The early stories of miracles by different saints tended to be associated with a specific place connected with the saint's life or death or with some relic; for example, how a monastery containing the tomb of a saint had been saved from destruction by his protection. Before the 11th century, local saints received more attention than Mary. Then, in the 12th century, the Virgin came to surpass all rivals. Since Mary was believed to have ascended into heaven, she had no earthly tomb; her power transcended geographical limitations, and her position as Jesus' mother identified her with all humanity.[3]

Mary's popularity owed something to pagan antecedents—to the mother goddesses of several religions; it also reflected the increased concern with women characteristic of the romances of the 12th century. Indeed, Mary was sometimes depicted as a jealous lover who demanded that men abandon their earthly mistresses for her service. A few of the miracles of the Virgin date from an earlier period and come from the Eastern church, one being the story of Theophilus given below. Most of them, however, grew up in the West and reflect the humanization of religion referred to above. As Eileen Power points out, the Virgin came to stand for "faith not for good works, for love not for justice. The medieval man felt that with her he always had a chance; he had only to believe in her and she would not desert him." [4]

The clergy as well as the laity encouraged the worship of the Virgin and often employed stories of her miracles in their sermons. The miracles related here are from a collection apparently designed for use in preaching. The compiler was a Swiss of the early 15th century who drew on a reservoir of stories current throughout the West. Although devotion to the Virgin became almost universal, it was probably nowhere more widespread than in England, which came to be called "Our Lady's Dowry."

Miracles of the Virgin Mary

In a certain convent of nuns many years ago there lived a virgin named Beatrice under vow of chastity. Devout in soul and a zealous servant of the Mother of God, she counted it her greatest joy to offer up her prayers to her in secret and, when she was made custodian, her devotion increased with her greater freedom. A certain cleric, seeing and desiring her, began to use enticements. When she scorned his wanton talk, he became so much the more eager, and the old serpent hotly tempted her, so that her heart could no longer endure the fires of passion, but going to the altar of the Blessed Virgin Mary, who was the patron saint there, she said: "Lady, I have served thee as faithfully as I could; behold I resign to thee thy keys. I can no longer withstand the temptations of the flesh." Placing the keys on the altar she went in secret after the cleric, and he, after dishonouring her, within a few days deserted her. And she having no means of living and being ashamed to return to the cloister, became a harlot.

Having lived publicly for many years in this wickedness, one day she came in her secular dress to the gate of the convent, and said to the gatekeeper: "Do you know one Beatrice, formerly the custodian of this convent?" And he replied: "Yes, she is a very worthy lady, holy and without reproach from her childhood, who has lived in this convent to this day."

She, hearing these words, but not weighing their meaning, was about to go away, when the Mother of Mercy appeared to her in the form of a woman and said: "For fifteen years I have filled your office in your absence. Return now to your home and do penance, for no one knows of your departure." The Mother of God had actually in her shape and dress taken her place as guardian. At once she returned, and as long as she lived gave thanks to the Virgin Mary, and in confession made known to her confessor all that had happened to her.

A certain abbot was caught in the midst of the British seas with others in a very great storm sent by God, so that all despaired of their lives. And so some were calling upon the Blessed Nicholas, some on the Blessed Andrew or any other Saint, for every one in his need invoked his own patron Saint in familiar terms.

But when the abbot saw them calling on these less powerful Saints, but no one naming the Mother of Mercy, who has power over heaven and earth and sea, he said: "What are ye doing, my brothers? Why do ye call on those Saints, who have less power, and omit one who has more power than all of them? Ye do indeed well, but ye would do much better if ye all with one voice acclaimed the Mother of Mercy."

Being thus counselled, all with one voice invoked the Mother of God, and all cried out to her to have pity on them. The abbot himself also, who had had nothing to eat except one apple, and who for two days and nights was in such sore distress that he could hardly draw breath, began with his monks to chant most earnestly the responsory: "Blessed, etc.," with its verse "Ora pro populo."

Scarcely had the people and the monks sorrowfully finished

the prayer with much devotion, when, behold, at the top of the mast a great light appeared like a candle, chasing away the darkness of night and flooding all in the boat with its brightness. And the storm ceased entirely on the sea, and at the command of the Queen of Heaven there was a calm. And not long after there dawned a fine day and the ship came to the land to which it was sailing.

There was a certain noble named Theophilus, who became impoverished and was at a loss what to do. At last he thought of going to the crossroads and talking with the Devil, to get him to aid in his worldly affairs. This he did, but when the Devil was besought with prayers by Theophilus to restore to him his wealth, he asked Theophilus if he could and would do what he proposed. He replied that he would, and took an oath. Going there three nights in succession, on the first night he renounced his baptism, on the second night his Creator, on the third even the Mother of Mercy.

But the Devil considering his love for the last, said: "If you will confirm this oath in an indenture written in your blood, then all is complete." This was accordingly done, the indenture written in the blood of Theophilus being confirmed by the Devil's seal.

It happened that one day Theophilus, stung with remorse, began to weep, and, as he wept, to prostrate himself before the image of the Blessed Virgin Mary, calling on the Blessed Virgin earnestly. But the Blessed Virgin was ever pitiful, and in her kindly pity for him she pardoned what he had done. And when Theophilus, prostrate before the altar, was weeping bitterly and praying to the image of the Blessed Virgin Mary, the image of God, as if in anger, would not listen to him and turned his face away.

Seeing this the Blessed Virgin placed her son's image on the altar and with Theophilus went to the Devil. Thus was he brought back to the grace of God and the Devil ordered by her to return the indenture of renunciation which Theophilus had given to him, and thus Theophilus was converted and at last entered into the joys of heaven.

The Mystery of the Redemption
(*14th or 15th Century*)

Like the theater of the ancient Greeks, that of medieval Europe grew out of the pageantry of religious worship. The Christian church, which had condemned and helped to destroy classical drama, in time gave birth itself to a form of liturgical drama in which the officiating clergy enacted stories from Scripture. Such dramatization of Scripture became known as mysteries (from the Latin word *ministerium,* meaning a church service). Similar presentations illustrating incidents from the legends of the saints are called miracle plays.

By the 14th century, mystery and miracle plays were acted outside of churches by guildsmen and in time by professional troupes of traveling actors. A number of English collections of these plays have been preserved and are known as the Chester cycle, York cycle, and so on, from the towns where they originated. The version of the *Redemption* given here comes, in abridged form, from a 15th-century manuscript obviously drawn from earlier sources.

The *Redemption* represents a mystery based on the life of Christ. By way of background, the first scene describes the Fall of man, thus explaining the necessity for human redemption. In the second scene Truth, Mercy, Justice, and Peace discuss with the Trinity man's fate. It is recognized that man can be saved only by God's sacrifice. At this juncture, God the Father calls on his Son to ordain some plan whereby man may win salvation. The selection opens with Christ's answer.

The Mystery of the Redemption

Christ:
   Father, He who shall do this must be god and man;
   Let Me see how I may wear that weed;
   And since in My wisdom he began
   I am ready to do this deed.
The Holy Spirit:
   I, the Holy Ghost, from You two proceed,
   Taking this charge at once on Me;
   I, Love, to Your lover shall give You speed:
   This is the consent of Our Unity.
The Father:
   Go, Angel Gabriel, as Our breath
   Into the country of Galilee;
   The name of the city is Nazareth;
   A wedded maiden you shall see
   The wife of Joseph, and verily
   She is of the house which David bore,
   The name of this maid of glee
   Is Mary, who shall all restore.
Christ:
   Say that she is sinless and full of grace
   And that I, the Son of God, shall be her son;
   Hasten that you may arrive apace,
   Or I shall be present ere you have begun.
   I have great haste to see this done,
   And to be born of a maid whom spirits adore.
   Tell her that by her is won
   All which your angels lost before.
The Holy Spirit:
   And if she ask how it may be,
   Tell her that I, the Holy Ghost, do this;
   She shall be saved through Our Unity,
   In token her barren cousin Elizabeth is

Quick with child in her old age ywis [indeed]
Tell her nothing is impossible for God to do.
Her body shall be filled with bliss
She shall soon believe this message true.

Gabriel:
On this high embassy, Lord, I shall fly,
It shall be done, even as a thought;
Behold, dear God, how true am I,
I take my flight, and linger not!
   [Gabriel *passes from heaven to the house of* Mary.]
Ave Maria, gratia plena. Dominus tecum.
Hail full of grace! God is with thee, I say!
Among all women blessed art thou!
Here the name Eva is turned to Ave,
That is to say, without sorrow, as thou art now.

Mary:
Ah, merciful God, this is a marvellous greeting!
The angel's words are dreadful to hear.
I am much troubled by this strange meeting,
Angels indeed daily appear
But not in form of man, and that is my fear,
Also to be given so high a name,
When I am unworthy of this heavenly cheer,
Gives me much dread and greater shame.

Gabriel:
Mary, for this have no dread,
For God's grace has fallen on thee.
Thou shalt conceive and in maidenhead
Bear the Son of the Trinity,
And Jesus His blessed name shall be.
He shall be great, the son of the highest, the angels' friend;
The Lord shall give him his father David's see,
Reigning in the house of Jacob whose reign shall have no end.

Mary:
Angel, I ask you now

In what manner this thing can be?
As for knowledge of man, I have none now;
I ever have kept, and ever shall keep, virginity.
I cannot doubt what you say to me
But I ask, so that I may know—
Gabriel:
From on high the Holy Ghost shall fall on thee
And the virtue of the Highest shall shadow so.
Of the holy Spirit thou shalt shortly bear
God's Son, who shall be called the Sapient One.
And see, thy cousin Elizabeth there
In her old age has conceived a son.
Her six months of bearing have run,
Her barrenness has passed away.—
Nothing is impossible which God will have done;
We listen to hear what thou wilt say. . . .

[*A pause.*

Mary:
With all meekness I incline to their accord,
Bowing down my face with all benignity.
See here the handmaid of our Lord:
According to thy word, be it done to Me!
Gabriel:
Gramercy, my lady free,
Gramercy for thy word of might,
Gramercy for thy great humility,
Gramercy, thou lantern of light!

[*Here the* Holy Ghost *descends with three beams of light to* Our Lady; *the* Son of God *shines with three beams upon the* Holy Ghost, *and* God the Father *with three beams upon the* Son. *And so all three enter her bosom.*

Mary:
Ah, now I feel in the body of me
Perfect God and perfect man;
And the form of a child's carnality
And all at once, thus God began.

I cannot tell what joy and bliss
I find through all my body fly;
Angel Gabriel, I thank thee for this;
Most meekly commend me to my Father on high.
Gabriel:
At thy will, Lady, it shall be,
Thou gentlest of blood, and highest of race,
Reigning on earth in any degree
Through the high occasion of heaven's grace.
I commend myself to thee, throne of the Trinity,
O mother of Jesus, and meekest maid!
Queen of heaven, lady of earth, empress of hell, these three
And succor of the sinful who cry for aid.
Through thy blessed body our bliss is remade,
To thee, mother of mercy, I humbly cry!
And as I began, with an Ave I fade,
Joining heaven to earth, and ascend on high.
   [*The angels in heaven sing the sequence: Ave Maria, gratia plena; Dominus tecum, virgo serena.*

Scene iv. The Cherry Tree

On the road to Bethlehem. A bare tree on one side of the stage. Enter Mary and Joseph traveling to Bethlehem.

Joseph:
Lord, what trouble is made for man!
Rest in this world is given to none
For our lord and Emperor Octavian
Demands a tribute from every one.
In every city the order's the same.
I, a poor carpenter of David's kin,
Must obey the commandment or fall in sin,
Coming to bitter blame.
Now, Mary, my wife, what have you to say?
For I must surely go from you

To the city of Bethlehem far away;
The journey is hard and the comforts few.
Mary:
My husband, I will take it too,
For there live some of my family.
Bethlehem is a city I long to view
And my friends will be a great joy to me.
Joseph:
Wife, I think of your baby; I greatly fear
That you would suffer crossing the wild.
You know I would gladly give you cheer,
Though women are moody whenever with child.
But come, let us go as fast as you may,
And Almighty God speed us upon our way.
Mary:
Ah, my sweet husband, what do I see?
What tree is standing upon that hill?
Joseph:
Why, Mary, that is a cherry tree;
At one time of year you might eat your fill.
Mary:
Look again, husband, more carefully;
Its blossoms are brighter than ever I saw.
Joseph:
Mary, come to the city speedily
Or we shall suffer the hand of the law.
Mary: Now, my husband, look once again.
How lovely cherries cling to the tree,
And though I would not cause you pain,
I wish you would pick a few for me.
Joseph:
I shall try to do what you desire.—
   [*He tries awkwardly to reach a branch, but fails.*]
Oh, to pick these cherries I won't be beguiled.
The tree is so high and I easily tire:
Let *Him* pluck your cherries who got you with child!

Mary:
>Now, good Lord, grant this boon to me,
>To have these cherries, if such is Your will.
>>[*The tree bows.*]
>
>Now I thank Thee, God; Thou hast bowed the tree
>And I may gather and eat my fill.

Joseph:
>Ah, I well know I have offended my God the Trinity
>In speaking to Mary so unkind a word as this,
>For now I believe it can only be
>That Mary bears the Son of the King of Bliss.
>May he help us in our need!
>You were nobly born of Jesse's race,
>Kings and prophets worthy of grace,
>And you worthy of your noble place,
>As learned men can read.

Mary:
>Thank you, husband, for what you say
>And first let us go on to our journey's end.
>Almighty Father, comfort us, I pray,
>And the Holy Ghost in glory be our friend.
>>[*They go out.*]

Scene v. The Adoration of the Shepherds

The Three Shepherds, Manfras, Bosenbace, *and* Mois, *lie on a hill. An* Angel *appears above. The manger, with* Mary, Joseph, *and* Jesus, *on the left.*

Angel:
>Joy to God Who reigns in heaven
>And peace to men on earthly ground!
>A Child is born to be your leaven;
>Through Him the folk shall be unbound.
>Sacraments there shall be seven
>Won through that Child's wound.

Therefore I sing to Him you believe in:
The flower of friendship now is found.
God, who rules the earth and sea,
Descends from heaven above to win
Man below and heal his sin,
Peace is come to all his kin
Through God's subtlety.

First Shepherd:

Manfras, Manfras, fellow mine,
I saw a light like silver shine,
I never saw so strange a sign
Shaped upon the skies.
Brighter than the sun's beam
On Bethlehem I saw it stream
And over all this region gleam,
Thrice I saw it rise.

Second Shepherd:

You are my brother Bosenbace;
I saw this miracle take place,
I know it is a sign of grace
Shining before dawn.
Balaam come to prophesy
A light should sparkle in the sky
When maid Mary's son should lie
In Bethlehem, new born.

Third Shepherd:

Though I love best silent joys,
A herdsboy whom men name as Mois,
In Moses' law I heard a voice
Calling on the cross.
Of a maid a Babe is born;
On a tree He shall be torn,
Saving folk who lie forlorn;
This Child shall heal that loss.

    [*Here the* Angel *sings "Gloria in excelsis."*]

First Shepherd:
    Eh, Eh, that was a wonderful note
    Which now was sung above the sky.
    I have the music all by rote. . . .
Third Shepherd:
    The song, I thought, retold the story,
    And afterwards I heard him say
    The Child that was born shall be Prince of glory
    And we should seek Him straightaway.
Second Shepherd:
    Let us follow with all our worth
    Going along with song and mirth
    To worship with joy at that blessed birth
    The Lord of all our throng.
    Let us march on speedily
    To honor that Babe worthily
    With mirth, song and melody.
            [*They arrive at Bethlehem.*]
    Now stay, and sing this song.
First Shepherd:
    Hail, Flower of flowers, the fairest found,
    Hail, Peerless pearl, the rose we prize,
    Hail, Bloom, by whom we'll be unbound
    With Thy bloody wounds in wondrous wise.
    To love Thee is my delight!
    Hail, Flower fair and free,
    Light from the Trinity,
    Hail, blessed mayst Thou be,
    Hail, Maiden, Mother of Might!

Act II

Scene i. Prologue of Satan

Satan *enters clothed as a young gallant. He addresses the audience.*

Satan:
  I am your Lord Lucifer; from hell I came;
  Prince of this world and great duke of hell.
  So Satan is now my rightful name.
  I come to hail you, and to greet you well.
  I am nourisher of sin to confusion of man;
  To bring him to my dungeon to dwell in fire.
  To reward my servant is my princely plan;
  He shall sing my sad praises in hell's choir.
  Pay good heed to your prince, my people dear;
  See what sports in heaven I dared to play.
  To win a thousand souls an hour is a trifle here
  Since I won Adam and Eve on the first day.

  But miraculous marvels move my remembrance.
  Of one Christ, called Joseph and Mary's son.
  Thrice I tempted Him with subtle dissemblance,
  Before His forty days' fast was fully done.
  He scorned to make bread of a barren stone;
  Angels aided Him on the temple's spire.
  His answers were more marvelous than moon or sun.
  I tempted Him to vainglory, but He foiled my desire.

  And now He has twelve disciples to attend Him,
  Whom He sends as servants to each city to find
  Proper provision and people to befriend Him;
  His miracles amaze the people's mind.
  He heals the lame, the halt, the blind;
  He raised up Lazarus, who lay four days in the grave.
  When I tempt a sinner, He comes at me from behind;
  Magdalene He dared to pardon and to save.

He pretends to be God's Son, born of a maid,
And says that He shall die for man's salvation;
That the trial of truth shall be no more delayed
When His body and soul have separation.
But those who are under my great domination
He can never rescue and drag from woe,
If a text hold true of God's own creation,
Quia in inferno nulla est redempcio.[5]

When the deadly day of His passion draws near
I shall rear new engines of malice and hate,
Contrive reproofs to put Him in fear
And have false witness to defame and berate.
His disciples shall leave Him in His sorry state.
A hundred wounds shall wrack Him, life and limb.
A murderous traitor shall determine His fate:
The rebukes that He gives me shall turn on Him.

See the ingenuity of my checkered disguise,
My garments fitting naturally together.
Each part correct in cut and size
From the sole of my foot to my bonnet's feather.
My long pointed shoes of the finest leather
With crimson stockings are my greatest joy;
My twenty points of lace tied with a silver tether
Make that gentleman yonder look like a boy.

I have long locks on my shoulders dangling down
To harbor live beasties that tickle men by night,
With a high bonnet for covering my crown;
I hold all beggars and poor men in despite.
In great oaths and lechery set your delight,
And maintain your estate by bribery and dinners;
If a law reprove you, say you will fight,
And gather a crowd of congenial sinners.

I have brought you new names where the old ones tire.
And since sin is so pleasant and each man's right,

You shall name pride honor, lust natural desire,
And covetousness wisdom, where money shines bright;
Wrath shall be called manhood, punishment called spite;
Perjury be a leader in each court or session;
Gluttony be called rest, abstinence be out of sight,
And all who preach virtue be put under repression.

The time is too short to name all my men
But all these shall inherit my eternal reign;
Though Christ may scheme, I shall put them into pen
Where they shall dwell with me forever in eternal pain.
Remember the mortal servants in my train;
For now I must leave you for others to play.
I shall be with you at all times when you call me again,
Only for a little while I go away.

The Priest and the Mulberries
(13th Century)

One form of popular medieval literature was neither aristocratic, like the epics and romances, nor primarily religious, like the miracle tales. Minstrels and other story-tellers related anecdotes of peasant and town life which often contained humor and usually drew some practical moral. Many of these *fabliaux* have no religious implications, but others, like *The Priest and the Mulberries,* afford an insight into the manner in which people saw the workings of the supernatural in almost any incident or accident of life. The story illustrates how closely the religious and the secular—the reverent and the irreverent—were intermingled in the life of the medieval man. The priest, though the divinely ordained agent of God, shares ordinary appetites and easily succumbs to temptation. The ridiculous calamity which befalls him shows how the laity loved to laugh at the clergy. Yet the story has a serious side: from his unfortunate experience the priest deduces two conclusions, one pragmatic, the other ethical.

The Priest and the Mulberries

A certain priest having need to go to market, caused his mare to be saddled and brought to his door. The mare had carried her master for two years, and was high and well nourished, for during these years never had she known thirst nor hunger, but of hay and of oats ever had she enough and to spare. The priest climbed to the saddle and set out upon his journey, and as well I remember that it was the month of September, for in that season mulberries grow upon the bushes in great plenty and abundance. The priest rode upon his way repeating his hours, his matins and his vigils. As he drew near the gate of the town the path ran through a certain deep hollow, and raising his eyes from his book the priest marked a bush thick with mulberries, bigger, blacker and more ripe than any he had ever seen. Desire entered his heart, for very covetous was he of this fair fruit, and gradually checking the pace of his mare, he presently caused her to stand beside the bush. Yet one thing still was wanting to his delight. The mulberries near the ground were set about with spines and thorns, whilst the sweetest of all hung so high upon the tree that in no wise could he reach them from his seat. This thing the priest saw, so in a while he climbed up, and stood with his two feet upon the saddle, whence by leaning over a little he could pluck the fruit. Then he chose the fairest, the ripest, and the sweetest of all these mulberries, eating them as swiftly and greedily as he might, whilst the mare beneath him moved never a whit. Now, when this priest had eaten as many mulberries as he was able, he glanced downwards, and saw that the mare was standing still and coy, with her head turned towards the bank of that deep road. Thereat the priest rejoiced very greatly, for his two feet were yet upon the saddle, and the mare was very tall.

"God!" said he, "if any one now should cry 'Gee up!'" He thought and spoke the words at the same moment, whereat the mare was suddenly frightened, and springing forward on the instant tumbled the luckless priest into the bush where the thorns and briars grew sharpest and thickest. There he lay in that uneasy bed, nor might move from one side to the other, backwards or forwards, for all the money in the mint.

The mare galloped straight to her own stable, and when the priest's household saw her return in this fashion they were greatly discomforted. The servants cursed her for an evil and luckless jade, whilst the cook maid swooned like any dame, for well she believed that her master was dead. When they were returned a little to themselves they ran to and fro, here and there, about the country searching for the priest, and presently on their way to the market town they drew near to that bush where their master yet lay in much misease. On hearing their words bewailing his piteous case, the priest raised a lamentable voice, and cried—

"Diva, Diva, do not pass me by. This bush is an uneasy bed, and here I lie very hurt and troubled and utterly cast down. Do you not see how my blood is staining these thorns and briars a vermeil red?"

The servants hurried to the bush, and stared upon the priest.

"Sir," said they, "who has flung you herein?"

"Alas," answered he, "tis sin has undone me. This morning when I rode this way reading in my Book of Hours, I desired over greatly to eat of the mulberries growing hereon, and so I fell into the sin of gluttony. Therefore this bush gat hold upon me. But help me forth from this place, for I wish now for no other thing but to have a surgeon for my hurts, and to rest in my own house."

Now by this little story we may learn that the prudent man does not cry aloud all he may think in his heart, since by so doing many an one has suffered loss and shame, as we may see by this fable of the Priest and the Mulberries.

Everyman
(*14th or 15th Century*)

The mystery and miracle plays were followed by a third type, the morality play, which was essentially an allegory. Moralities, likewise acted by guildsmen and by professional troupes, enjoyed a great vogue. One of the most popular was *Everyman*. The version presented here is based on an early 16th-century English translation of a Dutch version. The play certainly dates from at least a century earlier and originally may have been English.

Everyman explains in simple but dramatic allegory the church's theology regarding salvation through faith and works. Since Everyman, like the ordinary medieval person, possesses faith, the question of salvation hinges on works. Everyman discovers that without good works he cannot be saved, but his Good Deeds are overburdened by his sins. To release them he must go to confession and do penance. Wycliffe had already questioned this traditional belief; Luther would soon repudiate it.

Everyman

Here beginneth a treatise how the High Father of Heaven sendeth Death to summon every creature to come and give an account of their lives in this world, and is in manner of a moral play.

[*The* Messenger *enters.*

Messenger.
I pray you all give your audience,
And hear this matter with reverence,
   In form a moral play.
The Summoning of Everyman it is called so,
That of our lives and ending maketh show
   How transitory we be every day.

This matter is wondrous precious,
But the meaning of it is more gracious
   And sweet to bear away.
The story saith: Man, in the beginning
Watch well, and take good heed of the ending,
   Be you never so gay!
Ye think sin in the beginning full sweet,
Which, in the end, causeth the soul to weep,
   When the body lieth in clay.
Here shall you see how Fellowship and Jollity,
Both Strength, Pleasure, and Beauty,
   Will fade from thee as flower in May,
For ye shall hear how our Heaven's King
Calleth Everyman to a general reckoning.
   Give audience and hear what he doth say.

[*The* Messenger *goes.*

God speaketh:

I perceive, here in my majesty,
   How that all creatures be to me unkind,
Living, without fear, in worldly prosperity.
   In spiritual vision the people be so blind,
Drowned in sin, they know me not for their God;
   In worldly riches is all their mind.
They fear not my righteousness, the sharp rod.
   My law that I disclosed, when I for them died,
They clean forget, and shedding of my blood red.
   I hung between two it cannot be denied,
To get them life I suffered to be dead,
I healed their feet, with thorns was hurt my head.
   I could do no more than I did truly,
   And now I see the people do clean forsake me;
They use the seven deadly sins damnable
   In such wise that pride, covetousness, wrath, and lechery,
Now in this world be made commendable,
   And thus they leave of angéls the heavenly company.

Every man liveth so after his own pleasure,
And yet of their lives they be nothing sure.
The more I them forbear, I see
The worse from year to year they be;
All that live grow more evil apace;
Therefore I will, in briefest space,
From every man in person have a reckoning shown.
For, if I leave the people thus alone
In their way of life and wicked passions to be,
They will become much worse than beasts, verily.
Now for envy would one eat up another, and tarry not
Charity is by all clean forgot.
I hoped well that every man
In my glory should make his mansion,
And thereto I made them all elect,
But now I see, like traitors abject,
They thank me not for the pleasure that I for them meant,
Nor yet for their being that I them have lent.
I proffered the people great multitude of mercy,
And few there be that ask it heartily.
They be so cumbered with worldly riches, thereto
I must needs upon them justice do,—
On every man living without fear.
Where art thou, Death, thou mighty messenger?

[Death *enters.*

Death.

Almighty God, I am here at your will,
Your commandment to fulfil.

God.

Go thou to Everyman,
And show him in my name
A pilgrimage he must on him take,
Which he in no wise may escape,
And that he bring with him a sure reckoning
Without delay or any tarrying.

Death.

Lord, I will in the world go run over all,
And cruelly search out both great and small.
Every man will I beset that liveth beastly
Out of God's law, and doth not dread folly.
He that loveth riches I will strike with my dart
His sight to blind and him from heaven to part—
Except if Alms be his good friend—
In hell for to dwell, world without end.
Lo, yonder I see Everyman walking.
Full little he thinketh on my coming!
His mind is on fleshly lusts and his treasure,
And great pain it shall cause him to endure
Before the Lord, of Heaven the King.
Everyman,stand still! Whither art thou going
Thus gayly? Hast thou thy Maker forgot?

[Everyman *enters.*

Everyman.

Why askest thou?
Wouldest thou know? For what?

Death.

Yea, sir, I will show you now.
In great haste I am sent to thee
From God, out of his majesty.

Everyman.

What, sent to me!

Death.

Yea, certainly.
Though thou hast forgot him here,
He thinketh on thee in the heavenly sphere,
As, ere we part, thou shalt know.

Everyman.

What desireth God of me?

Death.

That shall I show thee.

A reckoning he will needs have
  Without any longer respite.
              Everyman.
To give a reckoning longer leisure I crave.
  This blind matter troubleth my wit.
              Death.
Upon thee thou must take a long journey,
  Therefore, do thou thine accounting-book with thee bring.
For turn again thou canst not by no way,
  And look thou be sure in thy reckoning,
For before God thou shalt answer, and show true
Thy many bad deeds and good but a few,
How thou hast spent thy life and in what wise
Before the Chief Lord of Paradise.
Get thee prepared that we may be upon that journey,
For well thou knowest thou shalt make none for thee attorney.
              Everyman.
Full unready I am such reckoning to give.
I know thee not. What messenger art thou?
              Death.
I am Death that no man fear,
For every man I arrest and no man spare,
For it is God's commandment
That all to me should be obedient.
              Everyman.
O Death, thou comest when I had thee least in mind!
  In thy power it lieth to save me yet;—
Thereto of my goods will I give thee, if thou wilt be kind,—
  Yea, a thousand pounds shalt thou get!—
And defer this matter till another day.
              Death.
Everyman, it may not be in any way.
I set no store by gold, silver, riches, or such gear,
Nor by pope, emperor, king, prince, or peer.
For, if I would receive gifts great,
All the world I might get,

But my custom is clean the contrary way.
I give thee no respite. Come hence, nor delay!
> *Everyman.*

Alas, shall I have no longer respite!
   I may say Death giveth no warning!
To think on thee, it maketh my heart sick,
   For all unready is my book of reckoning.
   But if I might have twelve years of waiting,
My accounting-book I would make so clear
That my reckoning I should not need to fear.
Wherefore, Death, I pray thee, for God's mercy,
Spare me till I be provided with a remedy!
> *Death.*

It availeth thee not to cry, weep, and pray,
But haste thee lightly, that thou mayest be on thy journey,
And make proof of thy friends, if thou can,
For, know thou well, time waiteth for no man,
And in the world each living creature
Because of Adam's sin must die by nature.
> *Everyman.*

Death, if I should this pilgrimage take,
And my reckoning duly make,
Show me, for Saint Charity,
Should I not come again shortly?
> *Death.*

No, Everyman, if once thou art there,
Thou mayest nevermore come here,
Trust me, verily.
> *Everyman.*

O gracious God, in the high seat celestial,
   Have mercy on me in this utmost need!
Shall I no company have from this vale terrestrial
   Of mine acquaintance that way me to lead?
> *Death.*

Yea, if any be so hardy
As to go with thee and bear thee company.

Haste thee that thou mayest be gone to God's magnificence,
Thy reckoning to give before his presence.
What, thinkest thou thy life is given thee,
   And thy worldly goods also?

Everyman.

I had thought so, verily.

Death.

Nay, nay, it was but lent to thee,
For, as soon as thou dost go,
Another a while shall have it and then even so,
   Go therefore as thou hast done.
Everyman, thou art mad! Thou hast thy wits five,
And here on earth will not amend thy life,
   For suddenly I do come!

Everyman.

O wretched caitiff, whither shall I flee
   That I may escape this endless sorrow!
   Nay, gentle Death, spare me until to-morrow
That I may amend me
With good advisement!

Death.

Nay, thereto I will not consent,
Nor no man respite, if I might,
But to the heart suddenly I shall smite
Without any "advisement."
And now out of thy sight I will me hie,
See that thou make thee ready speedily,
For thou mayest say this is the day
Wherefrom no man living may escape away.

Everyman.

Alas, I may well weep with sighs deep!
   Now have I no manner of company
To help me on my journey and me to keep,
   And also my writing is all unready.
What can I do that may excuse me!

I would to God I had never been begot!
To my soul a full great profit it would be,
    For now I fear pains huge and great, God wot!
The time passeth—help, Lord, that all things wrought!
For, though I mourn, yet it availeth naught.
The day passeth and is almost through,
I wot not well of aught that I may do.
To whom were it best that I my plaint should make?
What if to Fellowship I thereof spake,
And what this sudden chance should mean disclosed?
For surely in him is all my trust reposed—
We have in the world so many a day
Been good friends in sport and play.
I see him yonder certainly—
I trust that he will bear me company;
Therefore to him will I speak to ease my sorrow.
Well met, good Fellowship, and a good morrow!
                              [*Enter* Fellowship.
            Fellowship speaketh:
I wish thee good morrow, Everyman, by this day!
    Sir, why lookest thou so piteously?
If anything be amiss, prithee to me it say
    That I may help in remedy.
                Everyman.
Yea, good Fellowship, yea,
    I am in great jeopardy!
                Fellowship.
My true friend, show to me your mind.
I will not forsake thee to my live's end,
In the way of good company.
                Everyman.
That was well spoken and lovingly.
                Fellowship.
Sir, I must needs know your heaviness.
I have pity to see you in any distress.

If any have wronged you, revenged ye shall be,
Though I upon the ground be slain for thee,
Even should I know before that I should die.
> *Everyman.*

Verily, Fellowship, gramercy!
> *Fellowship.*

Tush! By thy thanks I set not a straw.
Show me your grief and say no more.
> *Everyman.*

If I my heart should to you unfold,
   And you then were to turn your heart from me,
And no comfort would give when I had told,
   Then should I ten times sorrier be.
> *Fellowship.*

Sir, I say as I will do indeed!
> *Everyman.*

Then you be a good friend at need.
I have found you true heretofore.
> *Fellowship.*

And so ye shall evermore,
For, in faith, if thou goest to hell,
   I will not forsake thee by the way.
> *Everyman.*

Ye speak like a good friend—I believe you well.
   I shall deserve it, if so I may!
> *Fellowship.*

I speak of no deserving, by this day,
For he that will say, and nothing do,
Is not worthy with good company to go.
Therefore show me the grief of your mind,
As to your friend most loving and kind.
> *Everyman.*

I shall show you how it is:
   Commanded I am to go a journey,
A long way hard and dangerous,

And give a strict account without delay
Before the High Judge, Adonai.
Wherefore, I pray you, bear me company,
As ye have promised, on this journey.
Fellowship.
That is matter, indeed! Promise is duty—
But if I should take such a voyage on me,
I know well it should be to my pain;
Afeard also it maketh me, for certain.
But let us take counsel here as well as we can,
For your words would dismay a strong man.
Everyman.
Why, if I had need, ye said
Ye would never forsake me, quick nor dead,
Though it were to hell truly!
Fellowship.
So I said certainly,
But such pleasant things be set aside, the truth to say;
And also, if we took such a journey,
When should we come again?
Everyman.
Nay, never again till the day of doom.
Fellowship.
In faith, then, will I not come there.
Who hath you these tidings brought?
Everyman.
Indeed, Death was with me here.
Fellowship.
Now, by God that all hath bought,
If Death were the messenger,
For no man living here below
I will not that loathly journey go—
Not for the father that begat me!
Everyman.
Ye promised otherwise, pardy!

Fellowship.

I know well I do say so, truly,
   And still, if thou wilt eat and drink and make good cheer,
Or haunt of women the merry company,
   I would not forsake you while the day is clear,
Trust me, verily.

Everyman.

Yea, thereto ye would be ready!
   To go to mirth, solace, and play,
Your mind would sooner persuaded be
   Than to bear me company on my long journey.

Fellowship.

Now, in good sooth, I have no will that way—
But if thou would'st murder, or any man kill,
In that I will help thee with a good will.

Everyman.

Oh, that is simple advice, indeed!
   Gentle Fellowship, help me in my necessity!
We have loved long, and now I am in need!
   And now, gentle Fellowship, remember me!

Fellowship.

Whether ye have loved me or no,
By Saint John, I will not with thee go!

Everyman.

Yea, I pray thee, take this task on thee and do so much for me,
As to bring me forward on my way for Saint Charity,
And comfort me till I come without the town.

Fellowship.

Nay, if thou wouldest give me a new gown,
I will not a foot with thee go.
But, if thou hadst tarried, I would not have left thee so.
And so now, God speed thee on thy journey,
For from thee I will depart as fast as I may!

Everyman.
Whither away, Fellowship? Will you forsake me?
Fellowship.
Yea, by my faith! I pray God take thee.
Everyman.
Farewell, good Fellowship,—for thee my heart is sore.
Adieu forever, I shall see thee no more!
Fellowship.
In faith, Everyman, farewell now at the ending.
For you I will remember that parting is grieving.

[Fellowship *goes.*

Everyman.
Alack! Shall we thus part indeed?
　Ah, Lady, help! Lo, vouchsafing no more comfort,
Fellowship thus forsaketh me in my utmost need.
　For help in this world whither shall I resort?
Fellowship heretofore with me would merry make,
And now little heed of my sorrow doth he take.
It is said in prosperity men friends may find
Which in adversity be full unkind.
Now whither for succor shall I flee,
Since that Fellowship hath forsaken me?
To my kinsmen will I truly,
Praying them to help me in my necessity.
I believe that they will do so
For "Nature will creep where it may not go."

[Kindred *and* Cousin *enter.*]

I will go try, for yonder I see them go.
Where be ye now, my friends and kinsmen, lo?
Kindred.
Here we be now at your commandment.
Cousin, I pray you show us your intent
In any wise and do not spare.
Cousin.
Yea, Everyman, and to us declare

If ye be disposed to go any whither,
For, wit you well, we will live and die together!
Kindred.
In wealth and woe we will with you hold,
For "with his own kin a man may be bold."
Everyman.
Gramercy, my friends and kinsmen kind!
Now shall I show you the grief of my mind.
I was commanded by a messenger
That is a High King's chief officer.
He bade me go a pilgrimage to my pain,
And I know well I shall never come again;
And I must give a reckoning strait [strict],
For I have a great enemy that lieth for me in wait,
Who intendeth me to hinder.
Kindred.
What account is that which you must render?—
That would I know.
Everyman.
Of all my works I must show
How I have lived and my days have spent,
   Also of evil deeds to which I have been used
In my time, since life was to me lent,
   And of all virtues that I have refused.
Therefore, I pray you, go thither with me
To help to make my account, for Saint Charity!
Cousin.
What, to go thither? Is that the matter?
Nay, Everyman, I had liefer fast on bread and water
All this five year and more!
Everyman.
Alas, that ever my mother me bore!
For now shall I never merry be,
If that you forsake me!
Kindred.
Ah, sir, come! Ye be a merry man!

Pluck up heart and make no moan.
But one thing I warn you, by Saint Anne,
  As for me, ye shall go alone!
Everyman.
My cousin, will you not with me go?
Cousin.
No, by our Lady! I have the cramp in my toe.
Trust not to me, for, so God me speed,
I will deceive you in your utmost need.
Kindred.
It availeth not us to coax and court.
  Ye shall have my maid, with all my heart.
She loveth to go to feasts, there to make foolish sport
  And to dance, and in antics to take part.
To help you on that journey I will give her leave willingly,
If so be that you and she may agree.
Everyman.
Now show me the very truth within your mind—
Will you go with me or abide behind?
Kindred.
Abide behind? Yea, that I will, if I may—
Therefore farewell till another day!
Everyman.
How shall I be merry or glad?—
  For fair promises men to me make,
  But, when I have most need, they me forsake!
I am deceived—that maketh me sad!
Cousin.
Cousin Everyman, farewell now, lo!
For, verily, I will not with thee go.
Also of mine own an unready reckoning,
I have to give account of, therefore I make tarrying.
Now God keep thee, for now I go!
                        [Kindred *and* Cousin *go.*
Everyman.
Ah, Jesus, is all to this come so?

Lo, "fair words make fools fain,"
They promise, and from deeds refrain.
My kinsmen promised me faithfully
For to abide by me stedfastly,
And now fast away do they flee.
Even so Fellowship promised me.
What friend were it best for me to provide?
I am losing my time longer here to abide.
Yet still in my mind a thing there is,
All my life I have loved riches.
If that my Goods now help me might,
He would make my heart full light.
To him will I speak in my sorrow this day.
My Goods and Riches, where art thou, pray?

        [Goods *is disclosed hemmed in by chests and bags.*
                Goods.

Who calleth me? Everyman? Why this haste thou hast?
  I lie here in corners trussed and piled so high,
And in chests I am locked so fast,
  Also sacked in bags, thou mayest see with thine eye,
I cannot stir; in packs, full low I lie.
What ye would have, lightly to me say.

                Everyman.

Come hither, Goods, with all the haste thou may,
For counsel straightway I must ask of thee.

                Goods.

Sir, if ye in this world have sorrow or adversity,
That can I help you to remedy shortly.

                Everyman.

It is another disease that grieveth me;
In this world it is not, I tell thee so,
I am sent for another way to go,
To give a strict account general
Before the highest Jupiter of all.

And all my life I have had joy and pleasure in thee,
Therefore I pray thee go with me,
For, peradventure, thou mayest before God Almighty on high
My reckoning help to clean and purify,
For one may hear ever and anon
That "money maketh all right that is wrong."
Goods.
Nay, Everyman, I sing another song—
I follow no man on such voyages,
For, if I went with thee,
Thou shouldest fare much the worse for me,
For, because on me thou didst set thy mind,
Thy reckoning I have made blotted and blind,
So that thine account thou canst not make truly—
And that hast thou for the love of me.
Everyman.
That would be to me grief full sore and sorrowing,
When I should come that fearful answering.
Up, let us go thither together!
Goods.
Nay, not so! I am too brittle, I may not endure,
I will follow no man one foot, be ye sure.
Everyman.
Alas! I have thee loved, and had great pleasure
All the days of my life in goods and treasure.
Goods.
That is to thy damnation, I tell thee a true thing,
For love of me is to the love everlasting contrary.
But if thou hadst the while loved me moderately,
In such wise as to give the poor a part of me,
Then would'st thou not in this dolor be,
Nor in this great sorrow and care.
Everyman.
Lo, now was I deceived ere I was ware,

And all I may blame to misspending of time.
Goods.
What, thinkest thou I am thine?
Everyman.
I had thought so.
Goods.
Nay, Everyman, I say no.
Just for a while I was lent to thee,
A season thou hast had me in prosperity.
My nature it is man's soul to kill,
If I save one, a thousand I do spill.
Thinkest thou that I will follow thee?
Nay, from this world not, verily!
Everyman.
I had thought otherwise.
Goods.
  So it is to thy soul Goods is a thief,
For when thou art dead I straightway devise
Another to deceive in the same wise
  As I have done thee, and all to his soul's grief.
Everyman.
O false Goods, cursed may thou be!
Thou traitor to God that hast deceived me,
And caught me in thy snare.
Goods.
Marry, thou broughtest thyself to this care,—
Whereof I am glad!
I must needs laugh, I cannot be sad!
Everyman.
Ah, Goods, thou hast had long my hearty love.
I gave thee that which should be the Lord's above.
But wilt thou not go with me, indeed?—
    I pray thee truth to say!
Goods.
No, so God me speed!
    Therefore farewell, and have good-day.
             [Goods *is hidden from view.*

Everyman.

Oh, to whom shall I make my moan
   For to go with me on that heavy journey!
First Fellowship, so he said, would have with me gone,
   His words were very pleasant and gay,
But afterwards he left me alone;
Then spake I to my kinsmen, all in despair,
And they also gave me words fair,
They lacked not fair speeches to spend,
But all forsook me in the end;
Then went I to my Goods that I loved best,
In hope to have comfort, but there had I least,
For my Goods sharply did me tell
That he bringeth many into hell.
Then of myself I was ashamed,
And so I am worthy to be blamed.
Thus may I well myself hate.
Of whom shall I now counsel take?
I think that I shall never speed
Till I go to my Good Deeds.
But, alas! she is so weak,
That she can neither move nor speak.
Yet will I venture on her now.
My Good Deeds, where be you?   [Good Deeds *is shown.*
        Good Deeds.

Here I lie, cold in the ground.
Thy sins surely have me bound
That I cannot stir.
        Everyman.

O Good Deeds, I stand in fear!
I must pray you for counsel,
For help now would come right well!
        Good Deeds.

Everyman, I have understanding
   That ye be summoned your account to make
Before Messias, of Jerusalem King.
   If you do my counsel, that journey with you will I take.

Everyman.
For that I come to you my moan to make.
I pray you that ye will go with me.
Good Deeds.
I would full fain, but I cannot stand, verily.
Everyman.
Why, is there something amiss that did you befall?
Good Deeds.
Yea, Sir, I may thank you for all.
If in every wise ye had encouraged me,
Your book of account full ready would be.
Behold the books of your works and your deeds thereby.
Ah, see, how under foot they lie
   Unto your soul's deep heaviness.
Everyman.
Our Lord Jesus his help vouchsafe to me,
For one letter here I cannot see.
Good Deeds.
   There is a blind reckoning in time of distress.
Everyman.
Good Deeds, I pray you help me in this need,
Or else I am forever damned indeed.
Therefore help me to make reckoning
Before him, that Redeemer is of everything,
That is, and was, and shall ever be, King of All.
Good Deeds.
Everyman, I am sorry for your fall,
And fain would I help you, if I were able.
Everyman.
Good Deeds, your counsel, I pray you, give me.
Good Deeds.
That will I do, verily.
Though on my feet I may not go,
I have a sister that shall with you be, also,
Called Knowledge, who shall with you abide,

To help you to make that dire reckoning.
>[Knowledge *enters*.
>>*Knowledge.*

Everyman, I will go with thee and be thy guide,
   In thy utmost need to go by thy side.
>>*Everyman.*

In good condition I am now in every thing,
   And am wholly content with this good thing,
Thanks be to God, my creator!
>>*Good Deeds.*

And when he hath brought thee there,
   Where thou shalt heal thee of thy smart,
Then go with thy reckoning and thy good deeds together,
   For to make thee joyful at heart
Before the Holy Trinity.
>>*Everyman.*

My Good Deeds, gramercy!
I am well content, certainly,
With your words sweet.
>>*Knowledge.*

Now go we together lovingly
To Confession, that cleansing river fair.
>>*Everyman.*

For joy I weep—I would we were there!
But, I pray you, give me cognition,
Where dwelleth that holy man, Confession?
>>*Knowledge.*

In the House of Salvation.
We shall find him in that place,
That shall us comfort by God's grace.
>[Confession *enters.*]

Lo, this is Confession. Kneel down, and ask mercy,
For he is in good favor with God Almighty.
>>*Everyman.*

O glorious fountain that all uncleanness doth clarify,

Wash from me the spots of vice unclean,
That on me no sin be seen!
I come with Knowledge for my redemption,
Redeemed with heartfelt and full contrition,
For I am commanded a pilgrimage to take,
And great accounts before God to make.
Now I pray you, Shrift, Mother of Salvation,
Help my good deeds because of my piteous exclamation!

Confession.

I know your sorrow well, Everyman,
   Because with Knowledge ye come to me.
I will you comfort as well as I can,
   And a precious stone will I give thee,
   Called penance, voice-voider of adversity.
   Therewith shall your body chastened be
Through abstinence and perseverance in God's service.
Here shall you receive that scourge of me
That is penance stronge, that ye must endure,
To remember thy Saviour was scourged for thee
With sharp scourges, and suffered it patiently—
So must thou ere thou escape from that painful pilgrimage.
Knowledge, do thou sustain him on this voyage,
And by that time Good Deeds will be with thee.
But in any case be sure of mercy,
For your time draweth on fast, if ye will saved be.
Ask God mercy, and he will grant it truly.
When with the scourge of penance man doth him bind,
The oil of forgiveness then shall he find.

                                                [Confession *goes.*

Everyman.

Thanked be God for his gracious work,
   For now will I my penance begin.
This hath rejoiced and lightened my heart,
   Though the knots be painful and hard within.

Knowledge.
Everyman, see that ye your penance fulfil,
  Whatever the pains ye abide full dear,
And Knowledge shall give you counsel at will,
  How your account ye shall make full clear.
Everyman.
O eternal God, O heavenly being,
O way of righteousness, O goodly vision,
Which descended down into a virgin pure
Because he would for every man redeem
  That which Adam forfeited by his disobedience—
O blessed God, elect and exalted in thy divinity,
  Forgive thou my grievous offence!
  Here I cry thee mercy in this presence.

O spiritual treasure, O ransomer and redeemer,
Of all the world the hope and the governor,
Mirror of joy, founder of mercy,
Who illumineth heaven and earth thereby,
Hear my clamorous complaint, though late it be,
Receive my prayers, unworthy in this heavy life!
Though I be a sinner most abominable,
Yet let my name be written in Moses' table.

O Mary, pray to the Maker of everything
To vouchsafe me help at my ending,
And save me from the power of my enemy,
For Death assaileth me strongly!—
And, Lady, that I may, by means of thy prayer,
In your Son's glory as partner share,
Through the mediation of his passion I it crave.
I beseech you, help my soul to save!

Knowledge, give me the scourge of penance;
My flesh therewith shall give acquittance.
I will now begin, if God give me grace.

Knowledge.
Everyman, God give you time and space!
Thus I bequeath you into the hands of our Saviour,
Now may you make your reckoning sure.
Everyman.
In the name of the Holy Trinity,
My body sorely punished shall be.
Take this, body, for the sin of the flesh.
As thou delightest to go gay and fresh,
And in the way of damnation thou didst me bring,
Therefore suffer now the strokes of punishing.
Now of penance to wade the water clear I desire,
To save me from purgatory, that sharp fire.
Good Deeds.
I thank God now I can walk and go,
And am delivered of my sickness and woe!
Therefore with Everyman I will go and not spare;
His good works I will help him to declare.
Knowledge.
Now, Everyman, be merry and glad,
Your Good Deeds cometh now, ye may not be sad.
Now is your Good Deeds whole and sound,
Going upright upon the ground.
[Good Deeds *rises and walks to them.*
Everyman.
My heart is light and shall be evermore.
Now will I smite faster than I did before.
Good Deeds.
Everyman, pilgrim, my special friend,
Blessed be thou without end!
For thee is prepared the eternal glory.
Now thou hast made me whole and sound this tide,
In every hour I will by thee abide.
Everyman.
Welcome, my Good Deeds! Now I hear thy voice,

I weep for sweetness of love.
Knowledge.
Be no more sad, but ever rejoice!
  God seeth thy manner of life on his throne above.
  Put on this garment to thy behoof,
Which wet with the tears of your weeping is,
Or else in God's presence you may it miss,
When ye to your journey's end come shall.
Everyman.
Gentle Knowledge, what do you it call?
Knowledge.
A garment of sorrow it is by name,
From pain it will you reclaim.
Contrition it is,
That getteth forgiveness,
Passing well it doth God please.
Good Deeds.
Everyman, will you wear it for your soul's ease?
        [Everyman *puts on the robe of contrition.*
Everyman.
Now blessed be Jesu, Mary's son,
For now have I on true contrition!
And let us go now without tarrying.
Good Deeds, have we all clear our reckoning?
Good Deeds.
Yea, indeed, I have them here.
Everyman.
Then I trust we need not fear.
Now, friends, let us not part in twain!
Knowledge.
Nay, Everyman, that will we not, for certain.
Good Deeds.
Yet must thou lead with thee
  Three persons of great might.

Everyman.
Who should they be?
Good Deeds.
Discretion and Strength they hight.
And thy Beauty may not abide behind.
Knowledge.
Also ye must call to mind
Your Five Wits as your counsellors beside.
Good Deeds.
You must have them ready at every tide.
Everyman.
How shall I get them hither?
Knowledge.
You must call them all together,
And they will hear you immediately.
Everyman.
My friends, come hither and present be,
Discretion, Strength, my Five Wits, and Beauty.

[*They enter.*

Beauty.
Here at your will be we all ready.
What will ye that we should do?
Good Deeds.
That ye should with Everyman go,
And help him in his pilgrimage.
Advise you—will you with him or not, on that voyage?
Strength.
We will all bring him thither,
  To help him and comfort, believe ye me!
Discretion.
So will we go with him all together.
Everyman.
  Almighty God, beloved mayest thou be!
I give thee praise that I have hither brought
Strength, Discretion, Beauty, Five Wits—lack I nought—

And my Good Deeds, with Knowledge clear,
All be in my company at my will here.
I desire no more in this my anxiousness.
Strength.
And I, Strength, will stand by you in your distress,
Though thou wouldest in battle fight on the ground.
Five Wits.
And though it were through the world round,
We will not leave you for sweet or sour.
Beauty.
No more will I unto Death's hour,
Whatsoever thereof befall.
Discretion.
Everyman, advise you first of all.
Go with a good advisement and deliberation.
We all give you virtuous monition
That all shall be well.
Everyman.
My friends, hearken what I will tell.
I pray God reward you in his heavenly sphere.
Now hearken all that be here,
For I will make my testament
Here before you all present.
   In alms, half my goods will I give with my hands twain,
In the way of charity with good intent,
   And the other half still shall remain
In bequest to return where it ought to be.
This I do in despite of the fiend of hell,
Out of his peril to quit me well
For ever after and this day.
Knowledge.
Everyman, hearken what I say.
Go to Priesthood, I you advise,
And receive of him in any wise
The Holy Sacrament and Unction together,

Then see ye speedily turn again hither.
We will all await you here, verily.
Five Wits.
Yea, Everyman, haste thee that ye may ready be
There is no emperor, king, duke, nor baron bold,
That from God such commission doth hold
As he doth to the least priest in this world consign,
For of the Blessed Sacraments, pure and benign,
He beareth the keys, and thereof hath the cure
For man's redemption, it is ever sure,
Which God as medicine for our souls' gain
Gave us out of his heart with great pain,
Here in this transitory life for thee and me.
Of the Blessed Sacraments seven there be,
Baptism, Confirmation, with Priesthood good,
And the Sacrament of God's precious Flesh and Blood,
Marriage, the Holy Extreme Unction, and Penance.
These seven are good to have in remembrance,
Gracious Sacraments of high divinity.
Everyman.
Fain would I receive that holy body.
And meekly to my spiritual father will I go.
Five Wits.
Everyman, that is best that ye can do.
God will you to salvation bring,
For Priesthood exceedeth every other thing.
To us Holy Scripture they do teach,
And convert men from sin, heaven to reach.
God hath to them more power given
Than to any angel that is in heaven.
With five words he may consecrate
God's body in flesh and blood to make,
And handleth his Maker between his hands.
The priest bindeth and unbindeth all bands
Both in earth and heaven.—

Thou dost administer all the Sacraments seven.
Though we should kiss thy feet, yet thereof thou worthy wert.
Thou art the surgeon that doth cure of mortal sin the hurt.
Remedy under God we find none
Except in Priesthood alone.—
Everyman, God gave priests that dignity,
And setteth them in his stead among us to be,
Thus be they above angels in degree.
Knowledge.
If priests be good, it is so surely;
But when Jesus hung on the cross with grievous smart,
There he gave out of his blessed heart
That same Sacrament in grievous torment.—
He sold them not to us, that Lord omnipotent.
Therefore Saint Peter the apostle doth say
That Jesus' curse have all they
Which God their Saviour do buy or sell,
Or if they for any money do "take or tell."
Sinful priests give sinners bad example in deed and word,
Their children sit by other men's fires, I have heard,
And some haunt of women the company,
With life unclean as through lustful acts of lechery—
These be with sin made blind.
Five Wits.
I trust to God no such may we find.
Therefore let us do Priesthood honor,
And follow their doctrines for our souls' succor.
We be their sheep, and they shepherds be,
By whom we all are kept in security.
Peace! for yonder I see Everyman come,
Who unto God hath made true satisfaction.
Good Deeds.
Methinketh it is he indeed.
Everyman.
Now may Jesus all of you comfort and speed!

I have received the Sacrament for my redemption,
And also mine extreme unction.
Blessed be all they that counselled me to take it!
And now, friends, let us go without longer respite.
I thank God ye would so long waiting stand.
Now set each of you on this rood your hand,
And shortly follow me.
I go before where I would be.
God be our guide!

Strength.

Everyman, we will not from you go,
   Till ye have gone this voyage long.

Discretion.

I, Discretion, will abide by you also.

Knowledge.

   And though of this pilgrimage the hardships be never so strong,
No turning backward in me shall you know.
Everyman, I will be as sure by thee,
As ever I was by Judas Maccabee.

Everyman.

Alas! I am so faint I may not stand,
   My limbs under me do fold.
Friends, let us not turn again to this land,
   Not for all the world's gold,
For into this cave must I creep,
And turn to the earth, and there sleep.

Beauty.

What—into this grave! Alas! Woe is me!

Everyman.

Yea, there shall ye consume utterly.

Beauty.

And what,—must I smother here?

Everyman.

Yea, by my faith, and never more appear!
In this world we shall live no more at all,
But in heaven before the highest lord of all.

Beauty.
I cross out all this! Adieu, by Saint John!
I take "my tap in my lap" and am gone.
Everyman.
What, Beauty!—whither go ye?
Beauty.
Peace! I am deaf, I look not behind me,
Not if thou wouldest give me all the gold in thy chest.
[Beauty *goes, followed by the others, as they speak in turn.*
Everyman.
Alas! in whom may I trust!
Beauty fast away from me doth hie.
She promised with me to live and die.
Strength.
Everyman, I will thee also forsake and deny,
Thy game liketh me not at all!
Everyman.
Why, then ye will forsake me all!
Sweet Strength, tarry a little space.
Strength.
Nay, Sir, by the rood of grace,
I haste me fast my way from thee to take,
Though thou weep till thy heart do break.
Everyman.
Ye would ever abide by me, ye said.
Strength.
Yea, I have you far enough conveyed.
Ye be old enough, I understand,
Your pilgrimage to take in hand.
I repent me that I thither came.
Everyman.
Strength, for displeasing you I am to blame.
Will ye break "promise that is debt"?
Strength.
In faith, I care not!
Thou art but a fool to complain,

You spend your speech and waste your brain.
Go, thrust thyself into the ground!
Everyman.
I had thought more sure I should you have found,
But I see well, who trusteth in his Strength,
She him deceiveth at length.
Both Strength and Beauty have forsaken me,
Yet they promised me fair and lovingly.
Discretion.
Everyman, I will after Strength be gone—
As for me, I will leave you alone.
Everyman.
Why, Discretion, will ye forsake me!
Discretion.
Yea, in faith, I will go from thee,
For when Strength goeth before
I follow after, evermore.
Everyman.
Yet, I pray thee, for love of the Trinity
Look in my grave once in pity of me.
Discretion.
Nay, so nigh will I not come, trust me well!
Now I bid you each farewell.
Everyman.
Oh, all things fail save God alone—
Beauty, Strength, and Discretion!
For when Death bloweth his blast,
They all run from me full fast.
Five Wits.
Everyman, my leave now of thee I take.
I will follow the others, for here I thee forsake.
Everyman.
Alas! then may I wail and weep,
  For I took you for my best friend.

Five Wits.
I will thee no longer keep.
  Now farewell, and here's an end!
Everyman.
O Jesu, help! All have forsaken me.
Good Deeds.
Nay, Everyman, I will abide by thee,
  I will not forsake thee indeed!
  Thou wilt find me a good friend at need.
Everyman.
Gramercy, Good Deeds, now may I true friends see.
They have forsaken me everyone,
I loved them better than my Good Deeds alone.
Knowledge, will ye forsake me also?
Knowledge.
Yea, Everyman, when ye to death shall go,
But not yet, for no manner of danger.
Everyman.
Gramercy, Knowledge, with all my heart!
Knowledge.
Nay, yet will I not from hence depart,
Till whereunto ye shall come, I shall see and know.
Everyman.
Methinketh, alas! that I must now go
To make my reckoning, and my debts pay,
For I see my time is nigh spent away.
Take example, all ye that this do hear or see,
How they that I love best do forsake me,
Except my Good Deeds that abideth faithfully.
Good Deeds.
All earthly things are but vanity.
Beauty, Strength and Discretion do man forsake,
Foolish friends and kinsmen that fair spake,
All flee away save Good Deeds, and that am I!

Everyman.
Have mercy on me, God most mighty,
And stand by me, thou Mother and Maid, holy Mary!
Good Deeds.
Fear not, I will speak for thee.
Everyman.
Here I cry God mercy!
Good Deeds.
Shorten our end and minish our pain,
Let us go and never come again.
Everyman.
Into thy hands, Lord, my soul I commend—
  Receive it, Lord, that it be not lost!
As thou didst me buy, so do thou me defend,
  And save me from the fiend's boast
  That I may appear with that blessed host
That shall be saved at the day of doom.
  In manus tuas, of mights the most,
Forever *commendo spiritum meum.*

[Everyman *goes into the grave.*

Knowledge.
Now that he hath suffered that we all shall endure,
The Good Deeds shall make all sure;
Now that he hath made ending,
Methinketh that I hear angels sing,
And make great joy and melody,
Where Everyman's soul shall received be!

[The Angel *appears.*

The Angel.
Come, excellent elect spouse to Jesu!
  Here above shalt thou go,
Because of thy singular virtue.
  Now thy soul from thy body is taken, lo!
Thy reckoning is crystal clear.
Now shalt thou into the heavenly sphere,

Unto which ye all shall come
That live well before the day of doom.

                     [The Angel *goes and the* Doctor *enters.*
                     Doctor.

This moral men may have in mind,—
  Ye hearers, take it as of worth, both young and old,
And forsake Pride, for he deceiveth you in the end, as ye will find,
  And remember Beauty, Five Wits, Strength, and Discretion, all told,
They all at the last do Everyman forsake
Save that his Good Deeds there doth he take.
But beware, if they be small,
Before God he hath no help at all,
None excuse for Everyman may there then be there.
Alas, how shall he then do and fare!
For after death amends may no man make,
For then Mercy and Pity do him forsake.
If his reckoning be not clear when he doth come,
God will say, *Ite, maledicti, in ignem æternum.*
And he that hath his account whole and sound,
High in heaven he shall be crowned,
Unto which place God bring us all thither
That we may live, body and soul, together!
Thereto their aid vouchsafe the Trinity—
Amen, say ye, for holy Charity!

                FINIS.
Thus endeth this moral play of Everyman.

NOTES TO CHAPTER IV

1. G. G. Coulton, *Five Centuries of Religion,* 4 vols. (Cambridge: Cambridge University Press, 1923-50), 1:156.

2. Quoted by Eileen Power in the introduction to Johannes Herolt, *Miracles of the Virgin Mary,* trans. C. C. Swinton Bland (London: George Routledge and Sons, 1928), p. xiii.

3. R. W. Southern, *The Making of the Middle Ages* (New Haven: Yale University Press, 1952), pp. 247-50.

4. Herolt, *Miracles of the Virgin Mary,* p. xxix. A Middle English version of Theoplilus expresses this faith as follows:

> Ther may no man ben so synful in thought,
> Whatsoever he hath myswrought,
> Good hope and trust he may haven
> That he schal fynde ever mercy
> Redly at Our Lady
> Yif he wil it of her craven.

Beverly Boyd, ed., *The Middle English Miracles of the Virgin* (San Marino, Calif.: Huntington Library, 1964), p. 87.

5. Because in hell there is no salvation.

CHAPTER V

The Disintegration of Medieval Society

THE LATTER HALF of the 14th century witnessed the weakening of many medieval institutions: the manorial system, monasticism, scholasticism. Forces themselves arising out of the medieval environment such as the strengthening monarchy and the growing towns, with their expanding trade and money economy, made change inevitable. The Great Schism, the Black Death, and the Hundred Years' War accelerated the rate of change.

Despite the popular piety illustrated in the last chapter, Englishmen manifested increasing discontent with the ecclesiastical establishment during the 14th century. The political character of the Avignonese papacy and the open division of the Great Schism undermined the church's prestige; Wycliffe and the Lollards questioned the need for the church hierarchy and the sacramental system. Writers like Langland and Chaucer, though more orthodox, ridiculed or denounced the worldliness of the clergy.

The Great Pestilence hit England in 1348-49, followed by lesser outbreaks during the next two decades. The population of the country was probably reduced by a third and did not fully recover until about 1500. As a result of the plague, an economic depression embraced most of western

Europe for a half century or more. The social dislocations which accompanied the catastrophe proved diverse. While some of the landed interests consolidated their position, most of the landlord class felt hard pressed because of a shortage of labor.[1] Parliament attempted to fix wages by means of statutory regulation. Most peasants probably experienced a rise in standard of living but there was much insecurity. Furthermore, the peasants resented parliamentary restrictions and were embittered by the wealth of the church and the great lay lords. The poll taxes of 1377, 1379, and 1380 precipitated an open revolt.

At first the Hundred Years' War had positive results. It awakened national feeling, and by requiring the king to seek new revenues, provided Parliament with an opportunity to increase its participation in government. The closing years of war, however, unhinged the political structure. The 1440s saw a failure of leadership. The crown in the hands of Henry VI was ineffective; the council became divided and incapable of administrating in his stead; Parliament had not reached a stage where it could direct the government. The French drove the English out of France, while in England a personal and factional struggle threatened to snap the political and legal bonds which held society together.

The following three selections illustrate in different ways the tensions and turmoil of the period. Langland's *Piers Plowman* voices both religious disillusionment and social criticism; Froissart's chronicle provides a graphic account of the Peasants' Revolt of 1381; *A Chronicle of Henry VI*, chosen from the mid-15th, reveals the disorder which ushered in the Wars of the Roses.

It is well to remember, nonetheless, that the closing years of the Middle Ages were characterized by growth as well as decay. The emergence of nationality, the increase in literacy (fostered by the foundation of grammar schools like Winchester and Eton), the birth of vernacular literature, the economic enterprise which made England into an exporter of cloth rather than raw wool—these and other developments demonstrate the vitality of the period.

A number of recent works have stressed the positive as contrasted with the negative aspects of English society in the later medieval era. A. R. Bridbury, in his *Economic Growth: England in the Later Middle Ages*,[2] challenges the emphasis placed by M. M. Postan and others on the population and economic decline. There has also been some revision in interpreting the political developments of the 15th century. George Holmes believes that the corruption of justice by the powerful was no novelty and that the system of mercenary retainers associated with the late feudalism originated much earlier.[3] W. H. Dunham argues that actually the mercenary retainers of the late 15th century were more a force for stability than a cause of insecurity,[4] while P. J. Helm sees the beginning of the modern state in the reign of Edward IV rather than in the Tudor era.[5]

Writing of the 15th century, C. L. Kingsford remarked: "there are everywhere signs of decay, and everywhere we encounter evidence of reconstruction on new lines. Morally, intellectually, and materially it was an age not of stagnation but of ferment: not indeed of achievement but none the less of promise."[6]

The Vision of Piers Plowman
(1377)

Neither the writings of the medieval clergy nor those of the aristocracy devote much attention to the life of the peasantry. Since peasants were generally illiterate as well as underprivileged, few records present their point of view. However, William Langland, the author of *Piers Plowman,* may well have sprung from peasant origins. From internal evidence in his work it has been inferred that he was the illegitimate son of a landed gentleman and a bondwoman. Born about 1332, Langland apparently attended a monastery school in Malvern, Worcestershire. As a young man he spent some time in London so that he knew urban as well as rural conditions. It is clear that Langland understood peasant problems and appreciated the bleak existence of the lower classes. He extolled the industrious poor but denounced beggars.

The Vision of Piers Plowman is an allegorical poem dealing with the theme of salvation. Langland's religious emphasis is on ethics. Like the author of *Everyman,* Langland believes that good works are essential to salvation. Unlike *Everyman, Piers Plowman* is social satire as well as allegory. In the poem the author describes many facets of English life, criticizing all classes yet displaying withal a respect for conventional values and the established order. The poem consists of a series of visions which come to Langland as he pauses to rest while walking through the Malvern Hills. The prologue offers a panorama of "all manner of men." The second selection below is from what is usually called the "Vision of Do Well," which contrasts the wickedness of men in many walks of life with the upright conduct they should perform. This section has more on the peasantry than any other part of the poem.

Three versions of *Piers Plowman* exist, dating from 1362, 1377, and the 1390s. The present translation is primarily based on the second. The fable of belling the cat found in the prologue dates

DISINTEGRATION OF MEDIEVAL SOCIETY

this text, since it must have been written just before the death of Edward III in 1377. In the fable the cat represents the king, the ratlings the nobles, and the mice the common folk. *Piers Plowman* enjoyed great popularity; over fifty manuscript copies of the poem still exist.

PROLOGUE

The Vision of the Field of Folk

Langland In a summer season, when soft was the sunlight,
I shook on some shreds of shepherd clothing,
And habited like a hermit, but not a holy one,
Went wide in this world, watching for wonders.
But on a May morning, on a Malvern hill-top,
A marvel befell me, as might a fairy-tale.
I was weary and far-wandered and went to rest myself
On a broadish bank, by a running brook,
And as I lay leaning and looking in the water,
I slipped into a slumber, it slid away so merrily.
 Then I began to move into a marvellous dream
That I wandered in a wilderness, would I could say where;
As I beheld into the East, high in the sunlight,
I saw a tower on a hill-top, of true workmanship,
A deepening dale beneath, and a dungeon within it,
With deep ditches and dark, and dreadful to see.
 A fair field full of folk, found I there between them,
Of all manner of men, the meaner and the richer,
Working and wandering, as the world asks of them.
Some were putting out to plough, had little play-time,
In setting seed and sowing, sweated at their labour,
Winning wealth that the worthless wasted in gluttony.
Some pranked themselves in pride, preciously apparelled,
Coming under colour of costly clothing.
To prayer and to penance many put themselves,

All for the love of our Lord living austerely,
In hope they might have their happiness in heaven,
Such as anchorites and hermits who hold to their cells,
And do not covet to go off gadding round the country
For bodily liking of a lecherous livelihood.
  And some chose business, with better achievement,
For it seems to our sight that such are successful.
Beggars and blackguards went busily about
With their bellies and their bags all brimming with bread,
Feigning sick for food, and fighting in the ale-house;
In gluttony, God knows, they go off bedwards,
And rise up with ribaldry, the knavish robbers,
Sleep and sorry sloth in hot pursuit of them.
  Pilgrims and palmers plighted themselves together
To seek shrines in Spain and sanctities in Rome.
They went on their way with many wise stories
And had leave to lie about it all their lives after.
I saw some that said they had been seeking saints;
In every tale they told their tongue was tempered to lie
Rather than to tell truth, it seemed from their talk.
  Hermits in a heap with hook-headed sticks
Went off to Walsingham, and their wenches with them,
Long lousy lubbers that were loth to labour.
I found the friars there, all the Four Orders,
Preaching the people for their private profit,
Gabbling about the gospel as seemed good to them,
Their money and their merchandize on the march together;
For since charity has been a cheap-jack in charge of confession,
Many a fine thing has befallen in a few short years.
  There preached a pardoner, as if he were a priest,
Dragging out documents with bishops' affidavits
And saying he himself could absolve them all
For having failed to fast, or being false to their vows.
Illiterates believed him and liked what he said,
Came up and crossed themselves, kissing his charters;

He bounced them with his brevets and bleared their eyesight
And they gave up their gold to gorge the glutton
For they trust these tricksters that trot after lechery.
Were the bishop awake, or worth his two ears,
His seal would never sanction this deceit of the people.
But it's not by the bishop that the bold boy preaches,
For the parish priest and the pardoner pocket the silver
Which the poor of the parish should have but for them.
  Parsons and parish priests complain to the bishop
That their parishes are poor since the pestilence time
Asking leave and license to live in London
And sing there for simony, for silver is sweet.
Bishops and bachelors and doctors of divinity,
Curates under Christ with the tonsure for token,
(Showing that they should be shriving their parishioners,
Preaching and praying for them and feeding the poor),
Lodge lazily in London all the long year.
Some serve the king, counting his silver,
In exchequer and chancery, challenging his debtors,
And some are in service to lords and ladies,
In the status of steward to step up their stipends;
Their masses and matins and many other services
Are undevoutly done, and I dread that at last
Christ at His coming may curse the whole lot of them.
I was conscious of the power in Saint Peter's keeping
To bind and to unbind, as the Bible tells us,
How he left it with love, as our Lord commanded,
Among the four virtues, best of all virtues,
That are called cardinal, closing the gateways
Where Christ is in kingdom, closing and shutting,
And opening to offer the happiness of heaven.
But of the cardinals at court, that catch at the name,
(Presumed to have power in appointing popes),
That they have Peter's power I do not impugn,
But in love and learning the election should lie.

So I can, yet I cannot, criticize that court.
  Then there came a king, accompanied by knighthood;
The might of the community made him their ruler.
Then came Common-sense, making men of learning,
To counsel the king and to save the community.
And common men managed, by manual craft,
And for the profit of all people, to ordain plowmen
To till and to toil, as a true life asks.
  Then there looked up a lunatic, a lean sort of fellow,
And kneeling to the king, he knowingly cried,

Lunatic "Christ keep you, Sir King, and all your kingdom,
And let you lead your land so that loyalty loves you,
And for your righteous rule be rewarded in heaven!"

Langland And then in air on high an angel of heaven
Launched into Latin—lest the illiterate
Should jabber and judge and justify themselves,
When they should suffer and serve—he therefore said,

Angel "*Sum Rex, sum Princeps, neutrum fortasse deinceps;
O qui iura regis Christi specialia regis,
Hoc quod agas melius, iustus es, esto pius!
Nudum ius a te vestiri vult pietate;
Qualia vis metere, talia grana sere.
Si ius nudatur, nudo de iure metatur.
Si seritur pietas, de pietate metas!*" [7]

Langland Then there glowered a grumbler, a glutton for phrases,
And to the angel on high instantly answered,

The Glutton for phrases
  "*Dum rex a regere dicatur nomen habere,
  Nomen habet sine re, nisi studet iura tenere.*" [8]

Langland And the common people caught it, countering in Latin,

The Common People
  "*Precepta regis sunt nobis vincula legis.*" [9]

Langland With that there ran a rout of ragged rats together
And little mice among them, more than a thousand,
And came to hold council for their common profit;

For a cat of the court, who killed for pleasure,
Leapt lightly over them and laid them low
Playing with them perilously and pushing them about.
Rats and Mice
"In doubt of his divers doings we dare but look at him;
And if we grumble at his games, he will grieve us all,
Catching us and clawing us, holding us in his clutches,
And life is loathsome till he lets us go.
If we did not want wit to withstand his will
We'd be the lords of life, and live at our pleasure."
Langland A rat of some renown, very ready with his tongue,
Said in suggestion of a sovereign remedy,
Rat "I have seen several," said he, "in the City of London,
Who bear bright bangles round about their necks;
Were there a bell on the bangle, by Jesu, it strikes me,
One would know when they were near, and nip away out of it!
So I reckon," said this rat, "that reason would lead one
To buy a bell of brass, or of brightest silver,
And clamp it on his collar for our common profit,
Noose it on the cat's neck, that we might hear and know
If he was roaming round or resting, or running out to play."
Langland And all this rout of ratlings ratified his reasons,
And then the bell was bought, and buckled on a collar;
But there was no ratling in all the rout ready to risk it
Or dared to bind the bell about the cat's bosom,
Or thread it round his throat, for the throne of England!
A mouse of some moment, as it seemed to me,
Struck out sternly and stood before them all,
And to the rout of ratlings rolled out his reasons:
The Mouse "Were we to kill the cat, yet there would come another,
To claw us and all our clan, though we crept under benches;
Therefore I counsel the community to let the cat be;
Better not be so bold as to show him the bell;

For I heard my sire say, seven years ago,
That where the cat is a kitten, the court is in trouble.
Holy Writ reckons (for those who can read it),
    Vae terrae ubi puer rex est, &c.[10]
Better a little loss than a long sorrow,
And the murder of a mouse than a general massacre.
Many a man has malt that we mice destroy,
And you, you rabble of rats, would rend a man's clothing,
Were there no cat at the court to catch and control you;
For if you rats had your way you could not rule yourselves.
And I say for myself," said the mouse, "seeing so far ahead,
Vex neither cat nor kitten, I can advise you.
No more babble about bells that are not worth buying;
Though it had cost me cash, I shouldn't care to touch it,
But would suffer the decisions of the cat in silence;
Collared or uncollared, let him catch what he can,
So I warn every wise one 'Look well to his own.' "

Langland There may be a moral to this, my merry men;
Guess it if you can, for by God I give it up!

  A hundred men were hovering like hawks, in silken hoods,
Serjeants-at-law, they seemed, in service at the bar,
And pleading at law for pounds and for pennies;
Never once for the love of our Lord did they loosen their lips.
You might better measure the mist on Malvern hill-tops
Than get a mumble from their mouths, unless money were
       shown them.
Barons and burgesses and bondsmen too
I saw in this assembly, as you shall see later,
Bakers and brewers and butchers galore,
Weavers of wool and weavers of linen,
Tailors and tinkers and tax-collectors,
Masons and miners and many other craftsmen,
All kinds of labourers alive, leaping out together,
Such as diggers and ditchers, doing an ill day's work,
Dallying through the long day with a "Darling, how goes it?"

Cooks and their kitchen-boys calling "Hot pies!
Good geese and gammon! Get a good dinner!"
Advertizing taverners told the same tale
With a "White Alsatian wine! Red wine of Gascony!
Rhenish and claret give relish to a roast!"
 All this I saw sleeping, and seven times more.

The Vision of the Pardon Sent by Truth

Truth heard tell of this and sent Piers word
To take out his team and till the whole earth,
And he purchased him a pardon, *a pena et a culpa*,[11]
For him and his heirs for evermore after.
All that helped him to harrow, or to set his seed,
Or try any trade that was trusty and useful,
Were put beside Piers in the pardon of Truth.
Kings and their council that keep the Church safe
And are righteous in their realm to the people they rule
Have a pardon that will pass them lightly through purgatory
To the fellowship in paradise of patriarchs and prophets.
Bishops that are blessed in being as they should be,
Legislators of two laws, "Love God," "Love your neighbour,"
And, inasmuch as they may, amending the sinful,
Are peers with the apostles, so the pardon showed,
And shall sit on the dais in the Day of Doom.
Some merchants, in the margin, were remitted many years,
But Truth sent them a letter, under secret seal,
That they should buy boldly and what they liked best
And sell it again, saving their winnings
For the help of hospitals, and those in poor health,
And for mending rough roads, a danger to many,
And building up bridges that were broken down;
They should find food for poor people in prison,
And send scholars to school or skilled occupation,

Truth   "And I shall send you myself Saint Michael my Archangel,
    That no devil shall dare to dismay you at death,
    But send your soul in safety to my saints in joy."
Langland   Then the merchants were merry and wept for delight
    And praised Piers the Plowman that purchased this pardon.
    Lawyers had but little, they litigate for money;
    The psalter does not save them, such as take reward
    Against the innocent especially, that have spared to do evil;
    The business of barristers should be to benefit,
    And princes and prelates should pay for their work.
    But he who spends his speech in speaking for the poor
    (If needy and innocent, and has injured none),
    Is showing the law for the love of our Lord
    And no devil at death shall dismay him a jot.

    All living labourers that live by their hands
    And take a just wage, having done a just work,
    Living in love and by law, with lowliness of heart,
    Have the same absolution as was sent to Piers.
    But there were no beggars in the bull of pardon,
    Save those who were driven, with reason, to do it;
    For he who badgers you with begging when he needs it not
    Is as false as the fiend, and defrauds the needy;
    Beguiling the giver against his will;
    For if he knew they were not needy, he would give it to another,
    Needier than they, and the neediest would be helped.
    He that begs borrows, bringing himself in debt,
    Borrowing on the security of God Almighty.

    The most needy are our neighbours, if we note it well,
    As prisoners in pits, and poor folk in hovels,
    Charged with their children and charged by their landlords.
    What they can spare from their spinning, they spend on the
            rent,
    And in milk and meal, to make a mess of porridge
    For the comfort of their kiddies, crying out for food.
    Also they themselves suffer much in hunger,

Wasting away in winter, and waking up of nights
Rising to rock an unruly cradle,
Combing and carding wool, patching old clouts,
Rubbing and reeling yarn, and peeling their rush-lights,
That pity it is to read of it, or put it into rhyme,
The woe of these women that work in such hovels
And of many another man, ground down in grief.
Thin with thirst and hunger, yet they turn the fair side outward,
And are abashed to beg, lest it be acknowledged
What they need from their neighbours, at noon and at even.
 Of all this I am well aware, for the world has taught me
How men are made to suffer that have many children,
With not a penny but their pittances to clothe and keep them
And many a mouth to fill, and few the pennies.
A loaf and a little ale, less than a pittance,
Cold fish or flesh, in place of roast venison,
And on Fridays and fasting-days, a farthing's-worth of mussels
Were a feast for such folk, or a few cockles.
This would be a charity, to help them, overcharged,
And comfort such cottagers, the crippled and the blind,
But for beggars with their bags, whose churches are breweries,
If they be not blind or broken, or bowed with illness,
Never care a rap, you rich ones, if such rascals perish.
And yet are there other beggars, apparently in health,
But wanting in their wits, both men and women,
Those that are lunatic, lolling and leaping,
Or sit about as mad as the moon, more or less.
They care not for the cold, nor take account of heat,
But move according to the moon; moneyless they wander,
With a good will, but witless, over many wide countries,
Just as Peter did and Paul, save that they preach not
And do no miracles; but many times it happens
That they utter prophecy, all as if in play;
God suffers such to go; and it seems to my judgment
They are his apostles, such people, or his privy disciples;

For he sent them forth, silverless, in a summer garment,
Barefoot and breadless, and they beg of none.
And though they were to meet the mayor in the middle of the street,
They do not reverence him, rather than another;
Neminem salutaveritis per viam.[12]
Men of this manner, Matthew teaches us,
We should have into our houses and help them when they come,
For they are merry-mouthed men, minstrels of heaven,
God's boys, the Bible says, jesters of Jesus,
Under his secret seal their sins are covered.
 But old men, hoary, helplessly feeble,
And women with child that may work no longer,
The blind and the bed-ridden and the broken-limbed
That being maimed are meek in all their maladies,
Have as plain a pardon as the Plowman himself;
For the love of their lowly hearts, our Lord has granted them
Their penance and their purgatory here on this earth.

A Priest "Piers," said a priest then, "I'll have to read your pardon,
For I will construe each clause into clear English."
Langland And Piers, at his prayer, unfolded the pardon.
Now I was behind them both and beheld this bull.
All in two lines it lay, not a leaf more,
Written and ratified by the hand of Truth:
 Et qui bona egerunt, ibunt in vitam eternam,
 Qui vero mala, in ignem eternum.[13]
The Priest "Peter!" said the priest then, "I can find no pardon,
But 'Do well and have well, and God shall have your soul,
And do evil and have evil, and hope for nothing better
Than that after your death-day the devil shall have your soul!'"
Langland And Piers in despair pulled the pardon in pieces,
Piers Plowman And said, *"Si ambulavero in medio umbre mortis,*
Non timebo mala; quoniam tu mecum es.[14]

I shall cease my sowing," said Piers, "and sweat no longer,
And be no more busy about my belly-joys!
Of prayer and penance my plow shall be hereafter
And weep when I should sleep, though wheaten-bread fail me.
Who loves God loyally, his livelihood is easy,
Unless Luke was a liar, who learnt from the birds.
We should not be too busy about the world's bliss,
'*Ne solliciti sitis,*'[15] he says in the Gospel,
Showing us by a parable how to shape ourselves.
The fowls of the field—who finds them meat in winter?
They have no garner to go to, but God finds for them all."

The Priest "What!" said the priest to Peterkin, "By Saint Peter, it seems
You have a little learning, aren't quite illiterate?"

Piers Plowman "Abstinence, the abbess, taught me my A B C,
And Conscience came later and taught me much more."

The Priest "Were you a priest, Piers," said he, "you might preach a sermon
As a doctor of divinity, taking for your text
Dixit insipiens."[16]

Piers Plowman
"You're a lewd lout," said Piers, "little you know the Bible!
Seldom have you seen the sayings of Solomon."

Langland The priest and Peterkin opposed each other
And with their words I awoke and waited about,
And saw the sun shining in a summer sky,
Meatless and moneyless in the Malvern Hills.
Marvelling at my vision, I moved into the valley;
  Many a time its meaning has moved me to study
All that I saw sleeping, and if it might be so.
Also for Piers the Plowman am I pensive at heart;
And what a pardon Piers had to comfort his people,
And how the priest impugned it with a couple of pert words.
And all this makes me meditate my vision,
And how the priest proved that Do Well gets no pardon;

Yet I deem that Do Well passes all indulgences;
Do Well at the Day of Doom shall be dealt with honour,
Passing all the pardon of Saint Peter's Church.
  Now the Pope has power to pardon his people;
This is our creed, and this the credential:
    Quodcunque ligaveris super terram, erit ligatum in coelis, &c;[17]
And so I believe loyally, Lord forbid otherwise!
Pardon and penance and prayer can save
Souls that seven times have done deadly sin.
But to trust in pardons truly appears to me
Less certain for the soul, surely, than Do Well.
  At the dreadful day when the dead shall arise
And all come before Christ to render their account,
How you led your life here, looking to His Law,
And how, day by day, you did, will then be dealt with;
A pocket-full of pardon there, and patents from the pope,
And indulgences redoubled . . . unless Do Well helps you,
I set your patents and your pardons at the price of an old
    pie-crust!
  So I counsel all Christians to cry God mercy.
May Mary, His Mother, be our mediator,
That God give us grace here, ere going hence,
That after the day of our death, at the Day of Judgment,
Do Well may declare we did as he commanded.

Froissart's Account of the Peasants' Revolt
(1410)

The Chronicles of England, France and Spain by Sir Jean Froissart is one of the best written of all medieval chronicles. Froissart was born at Valenciennes in France in 1337. He came to England as secretary to Phillipa of Hainault, wife of Edward III. Froissart attended the courts of Scotland and Brabant as well as that of England and traveled extensively. Most of his chronicle deals with different aspects of the Hundred Years' War and concerns itself chiefly with the court and the nobility. The events of 1381 clearly represent an unwelcome intrusion of plebeian life into Froissart's world of tourneys, battles, and diplomatic intrigue. He finished the first two parts of his history in 1388, while living in Flanders; he completed the work sometime after 1390. The date of his death remains uncertain but appears to have been about 1410.

The passages in *Piers Plowman* describing peasant conditions help to explain the background of the revolt of 1381. *Piers Plowman* itself was known to some of the rebel leaders. John Ball wrote a letter to Wat Tyler's followers bidding "Piers Plowman go to his work." The teachings of the Lollards also contributed to the unrest among the peasants. Yet the authorities seem to have been taken unawares by the outbreak. "It would be difficult to exaggerate the air of helpless bewilderment with which the governing classes greeted the events of June 1381." [18]

The Peasants' Revolt

While these conferences were going forward there happened great commotions among the lower orders in England, by which that country was nearly ruined. In order that this disastrous rebellion may serve as an example to mankind, I will speak of all that was done from the information I had at the time. It is customary in England, as well as in several other countries, for the nobility to have great privileges over the commonalty; that is to say, the lower orders are bound by law to plough the lands of the gentry, to harvest their grain, to carry it home to the barn, to thrash and winnow it; they are also bound to harvest and carry home the hay. All these services the prelates and gentlemen exact of their inferiors; and in the counties of Kent

Essex, Sussex, and Bedford, these services are more oppressive than in other parts of the kingdom. In consequence of this the evil-disposed in these districts began to murmur, saying, that in the beginning of the world there were no slaves, and that no one ought to be treated as such, unless he had committed treason against his lord, as Lucifer had done against God; but they had done no such thing, for they were neither angels nor spirits, but men formed after the same likeness as these lords who treated them as beasts. This they would bear no longer; they were determined to be free, and if they laboured or did any work, they would be paid for it. A crazy priest in the county of Kent, called John Ball, who for his absurd preaching had thrice been confined in prison by the Archbishop of Canterbury, was greatly instrumental in exciting these rebellious ideas. Every Sunday after mass, as the people were coming out of church, this John Ball was accustomed to assemble a crowd around him in the marketplace and preach to them. On such occasions he would say, "My good friends, matters cannot go on well in England until all things shall be in common; when there shall be neither vassals nor lords; when the lords shall be no more masters than ourselves. How ill they behave to us! for what reason do they thus hold us in bondage? Are we not all descended from the same parents, Adam and Eve? And what can they show, or what reason can they give, why they should be more masters than ourselves? They are clothed in velvet and rich stuffs, ornamented with ermine and other furs, while we are forced to wear poor clothing. They have wines, spices, and fine bread, while we have only rye and the refuse of the straw; and when we drink, it must be water. They have handsome seats and manors, while we must brave the wind and rain in our labours in the field; and it is by our labour they have wherewith to support their pomp. We are called slaves, and if we do not perform our service we are beaten, and we have no sovereign to whom we can complain or who would be willing to hear us. Let us go to the king and remonstrate with him; he is young, and from him we may obtain a favourable answer, and if not we must ourselves seek to amend our condition." With such language as this did John Ball harangue the people of his village every Sunday after mass. The archbishop, on being informed of it, had him arrested and imprisoned for two or three months by way of punishment; but the moment he was out of prison, he returned to his former course. Many in the city of London envious of the rich and noble, having heard of John Ball's preaching, said among themselves that the country was badly governed, and that the nobility had seized upon all the gold and silver. These wicked Londoners, therefore, began to assemble in parties, and to show signs of rebellion; they also invited all those who held like opinions in the adjoining counties to come to London; telling them that they would find the town open to them and the commonalty of the same way of thinking as themselves, and that they would so press the king, that there should no longer be a slave in England.

By this means the men of Kent, Essex, Sussex, Bedford, and the adjoining counties, in number about 60,000, were brought to London, under command of Wat Tyler, Jack Straw, and John Ball. This Wat Tyler, who was chief of the three, had been a tiler of houses—a bad man and a great enemy to the nobility. When these wicked people first began their disturbances, all London, with the exception of those who favoured them, was much alarmed. The mayor and rich citizens assembled in council and debated whether they should shut the gate and refuse to admit them; however, upon mature reflection they determined not to do so, as they might run the risk of having the suburbs burnt. The gates of the city were therefore thrown open, and the rabble entered and lodged as they pleased. True it is that full two-thirds of these people knew neither what they wanted, nor for what purpose they had come together; they followed one another like sheep. In this manner did many of these poor fellows walk to London from distances of one hundred, or sixty leagues, but the greater part came from the counties I have mentioned, and all on their arrival demanded to see the king. The country gentlemen, the knights and squires, began to be much alarmed when they saw the people thus assembling, and indeed they had sufficient reason to be so, for far less causes have excited fear. As the Kentish rebels were on their road towards London, the Princess of Wales, the king's mother, was returning from a pilgrimage to Canterbury; and when they saw her the scoundrels attacked her car and caused the good lady much alarm; but God preserved her from violence, and she came the whole journey from Canterbury to London without venturing to make any stoppage. On her arrival in London, King Richard was at the Tower; thither then the princess went immediately, and found the king, attended by the Earl of Salisbury, the Archbishop of Canterbury, Sir Robert de Namur, and several others, who had kept near his person from suspicion of the rebels. King Richard well knew that this rebellion was in agitation long before it broke out, and it was a matter of astonishment to every one that he attempted to apply no remedy.

In order that gentlemen and others may take example and learn to correct such wicked rebels, I will most amply detail how the whole business was conducted. On the Monday preceding the feast of the Holy Sacrament in the year 1381, these people sallied forth from their homes to come to London, intending, as they said, to remonstrate with the king, and to demand their freedom. At Canterbury, they met John Ball, Wat Tyler, and Jack Straw. On entering this city they were well feasted by the inhabitants, who were all of the same way of thinking as themselves; and having held a council there, resolved to proceed on their march to London. They also sent emissaries across the Thames into Essex, Suffolk, and Bedford, to press the people of these parts to do the same, in order that the city might be quite surrounded. It was the intention of the leaders of this rabble, that all the different parties should be collected on the feast of the Holy Sacrament on the day following. At Canterbury the rebels entered the church of St. Thomas, where they did much damage; they also pillaged the apartments of the archbishop, saying as they were carrying off the different articles, "The Chancellor of England has had this piece of furniture very cheap; he must now give us an account of his revenues, and of the large sums which he has levied since the coronation of the king." After this they plundered the abbey of St. Vincent, and then leaving Canterbury took the road towards Rochester. As they passed they collected people from the villages right and left, and on they went like a tempest, destroying all the houses belonging to attorneys, king's proctors, and the archbishop, which came in their way. At Rochester they met with the same welcome as at Canterbury, for all the people were anxious to join them. Here they went at once to the castle, and seizing a knight by name Sir John de Newtoun, who was constable of the castle and captain of the town, told him that he must accompany them as their commander-in-chief and do whatever they wished. The knight endeavoured to excuse himself; but they met his excuses by saying, "Sir John, if you refuse you are a dead man." Upon which, finding that the outrageous mob were ready to kill him, he was constrained to comply with their request.

In other counties of England the rebels acted in a similar manner, and several great lords and knights, such as the Lord Manley, Sir Stephen Hales, and Sir Thomas Cossington, were compelled to march with them. Now observe how fortunately matters turned out, for had these scoundrels succeeded in their intentions, all the nobility of England would have been destroyed; and after such success as this the people of other nations would have rebelled also, taking example from those of Ghent and Flanders, who at the time were in actual rebellion against their lord; the Parisians indeed the same year acted in a somewhat similar manner; upwards of 20,000 of them armed themselves with leaden maces and caused a rebellion, which I shall speak of as we go on; but I must first finish my account of these disturbances in England. When the rebels had done all they wanted at Rochester, they left that city and came to Dartford, continuing to destroy all the houses of lawyers and proctors on the right and left of the road; from Dartford they came to Blackheath, where they took up their quarters, saying, that they were armed for the king and commons of England. When the principal citizens of London found that the rebels were quartered so near them, they caused the gates of London-bridge to be closed, and placed guards there, by order of Sir William Walworth, Mayor of London; notwithstanding there were in the city more than 30,000 who favoured the insurgents. Information that the gates of London-bridge had been closed against them soon reached Blackheath, whereupon the rebels sent a knight to speak with the king and to tell him that what they were doing was for his service; for the kingdom had now for many years been wretchedly governed, to the great dishonour of the realm and to the oppression of the lower orders of the people, by his uncles, by the clergy, and more especially by the Archbishop of Canterbury, his chancellor, from whom they were determined to have an account of his ministry. The knight who was appointed to this service would willingly have excused himself, but he did not dare to do it; so advancing to the Thames opposite the Tower, he took a boat and crossed over. The king and those who were with him in the Tower were in the greatest possible suspense and most anxious to receive some intelligence when the knight's arrival was announced, who was immediately conducted into the royal presence. With the king at this time were the princess his mother, his two natural brothers, the Earl of Kent and Sir John Holland, the Earls of Salisbury, Warwick, and Suffolk, the Archbishop of Canterbury, the great Prior of the Templars, Sir Robert de Namur, the Mayor of London, and several of the principal citizens. Immediately upon entering the apartment the knight cast himself on his knees before the king, saying, "My much redoubted lord, do not be displeased with me for the message which I am about to deliver to you; for, my dear lord, I have been compelled to come hither." "By no means, sir knight," said the king. "Tell us what you are charged with, we hold you excused." "My most redoubted lord, the commons of this realm have sent me to entreat you to come to Blackheath and speak with them. They wish to have no one but yourself: and you need not fear for your person, as they will not do you the least harm; they always have respected you as their king, and will continue to do so; but they desire to tell you many things which they say it is necessary you should hear: with these, however, they have not empowered me to make you acquainted. Have the goodness, dear lord, to give me such an answer as may satisfy them, and that they may be convinced that I have really been in your presence; for they have my children as hostages for my return, and if I go not back they will assuredly put them to death." To this the king merely replied, "You shall have my answer speedily"; and when the knight had withdrawn, he desired his council to consider what was to be done; after some consultation, the king was advised to send word to the insurgents, that if on Thursday they would come down to the river Thames, he would without fail speak with them. The knight on receiving this answer was well satisfied, and taking leave of the king and his barons, returned to Blackheath, where upwards of 60,000 men were assembled. He told them from the king, that if they would send their leaders the next morning to the Thames, the king would come and hear what they had to say. The answer was deemed satisfactory; and the rebels passed the night as well as they could, but you must know that one-fourth of them were without provisions.

At this time the Earl of Buckingham was in Wales, where he possessed large estates in right of his wife; and the common report in London was, that he favoured these people: some asserted it for a truth, declaring that they had seen him among them, for there was one Thomas from Cambridge who very much resembled him. The English barons who were at Plymouth, preparing for their voyage, when they heard of the rebellion were fearful lest they should be prevented, and consequently as soon as they could weighed anchor and put to sea. The Duke of

Lancaster, who was on the borders between Morlane, Roxburgh, and Melrose, holding conferences with the Scots, also received intelligence of the rebellion, and of the danger he was in, for he well knew his own unpopularity. Notwithstanding this, he managed very satisfactorily his treaty with the Scottish commissioners, who themselves also knew what was going on in England, and how the populace were everywhere rising against the nobility. But to return to the commonalty of England: on Corpus Christi day King Richard heard mass in the Tower of London, after which he entered his barge, attended by the Earls of Salisbury, Warwick, and Suffolk, and some other knights, and rowed down the Thames towards Rotherhithe, a royal manor, where upwards of 10,000 of the insurgents had assembled. As soon as the mob perceived the royal barge approaching, they began shouting and crying as if all the spirits of the nether world had been in the company. With them, also, was the knight whom they had sent to the Tower to the king; for if the king had not come, they determined to have him cut to pieces, as they had threatened him.

When the king and his lords saw this crowd of people, and the wildness of their manner, the boldest of the party felt alarm, and the king was advised not to land, but to have his barge rowed up and down the river. "What do you wish for?" he demanded of the multitude; "I am come hither to hear what you have to say." Those near him cried out, "We wish you to land, and then we will tell you what our wants are." Upon this the Earl of Salisbury cried out, "Gentlemen, you are not properly dressed, nor are you in a fit condition for a king to talk with." Nothing more was said on either side, for the king was prevailed upon at once to return to the Tower. The people seeing this were in a great passion, and returned to Blackheath to inform their companions how the king had served them; upon hearing which, they all cried out, "Let us instantly march to London." Accordingly they set out at once, and on the road thither destroyed all the houses of lawyers and courtiers, and all the monasteries they met with. In the suburbs of London, which are very handsome and extensive, they pulled down many fine houses: they demolished also the king's prison, called the Marshalsea, and set at liberty all who were confined in it; moreover, they threatened the Londoners at the entrance of the bridge for having shut the gates of it, declaring that they would take the city by storm, and afterwards burn and destroy it.

With regard to the common people of London, numbers entertained these rebellious opinions, and on assembling at the bridge asked of the guards, "Why will you refuse admittance to these honest men? they are our friends, and what they are doing is for our good." So urgent were they, that it was found necessary to open the gates, when crowds rushed in and took possession of those shops which seemed best stocked with provisions; indeed, wherever they went, meat and drink were placed before them, and nothing was refused in the hope of appeasing them. Their leaders, John Ball, Jack Straw, and Wat Tyler, then marched through London, attended by more than 20,000 men, to the palace of the Savoy, which is a handsome building belonging to the Duke of Lancaster, situated on the banks of the Thames on the road to Westminster: here they immediately killed the porters, pushed into the house, and set it on fire. Not content with this outrage, they went to the house of the Knight-hospitalers of Rhodes, dedicated to St. John of Mount Carmel, which they burnt together with their church and hospital.

After this they paraded the streets, and killed every Fleming they could find, whether in house, church, or hospital: they broke open several houses of the Lombards, taking whatever money they could lay their hands upon. They murdered a rich citizen, by name Richard Lyon, to whom Wat Tyler had formerly been servant in France, but having once beaten him, the varlet had never forgotten it; and when he had carried his men to his house, he ordered his head to be cut off, placed upon a pike, and carried through the streets of London. Thus did these wicked people act, and on this Thursday they did much damage to the city of London. Towards evening they fixed their quarters in a square, called St. Catherine's, before the Tower, declaring that they would not depart until they had obtained from the king everything they wanted—until the Chancellor of England had accounted to them, and shown how the great sums which were raised had been expended. Considering the mischief which the mob had already done, you may easily imagine how miserable, at this time, was the situation of the king and those who were with him. In the evening, he and his barons, together with Sir William Walworth, and some of the principal citizens, held a council in the Tower, when it was proposed to arm themselves and fall by night upon these wretches while they were drunk and asleep, for they might have been killed like so many fleas, as not one of them in twenty had arms: and the citizens were very capable of doing this, for they had secretly received into their house their friends and servants properly prepared for action. Sir Robert Knolles remained in his house guarding it, with more than six-score companions completely armed, who could have sallied forth at a minute's notice. Sir Perducas d'Albret was also in London at this period, and would of course have been of great service, so that altogether they could have mustered upwards of 8,000 men well armed. However, nothing was done; they were really too much afraid of the commonalty; and the king's advisers, the Earl of Salisbury and others, said to him, "Sir, if you can appease them by fair words, it will be so much the better; for should we begin what we cannot go through, it will be all over with us and our heirs, and England will be a desert." This counsel was followed, and the mayor ordered to make no stir; who obeyed, as in reason he ought. On Friday morning the rebels, who lodged in the square of St. Catherine's, before the Tower, began to make themselves ready. They shouted much and said, that if the king would not come out to them, they would attack the Tower, storm it, and slay all who were within. The king, alarmed at these menaces, resolved to speak with the rabble; he therefore sent orders for them to retire to a handsome meadow at Mile-end, where, in the summertime, people go to amuse themselves, at the same time signifying that he would meet them there and grant their demands. Proclamation to this effect was made in the king's name, and thither, accordingly, the commonalty of the different villages began to march; many, however, did not care to go, but stayed behind in London, being more desirous of the riches of the nobles and the plunder of the city. Indeed, covetousness and the desire of plunder was the principal cause of these disturbances, as the rebels showed very plainly. When the gates of the Tower were thrown open, and the king attended by his two brothers and other nobles had passed through, Wat Tyler, Jack Straw, and John Ball, with upwards of 400 others, rushed in by force, and running from chamber to chamber, found the Archbishop of Canterbury, by name Simon, a valiant and wise man, whom the rascals seized and beheaded.[19] The prior of St. John's suffered the same fate, and likewise a Franciscan friar, a doctor of physic, who was attached to the Duke of Lancaster, also a sergeant-at-arms, whose name was John Laige.

The heads of these four persons the rebels fixed on long spikes and had them carried before them through the streets of London; and when they had made sufficient mockery of them, they caused them to be placed on London-bridge, as if they had been traitors to their king and country. The scoundrels then entered the apartment of the princess and cut her bed to pieces, which so terrified her that she fainted, and in this condition she was carried by her servants and ladies to the river side, when she was put into a covered boat and conveyed to a house called the Wardrobe, where she continued for a day and night in a very precarious state. While the king was on his way to Mile-end, his two brothers, the Earl of Kent and Sir John Holland, stole away from his company, not daring to show themselves to the populace. The king himself, however, showed great courage, and on his arrival at the appointed spot instantly advanced into the midst of the assembled multitude, saying in a most pleasing manner, "My good people, I am your king and your lord, what is it you want?

What do you wish to say to me?" Those who heard him made answer, "We wish you to make us free for ever. We wish to be no longer called slaves, nor held in bondage." The king replied, "I grant your wish; now therefore return to your homes, and let two or three from each village be left behind, to whom I will order letters to be given with my seal, fully granting every demand you have made: and in order that you may be the more satisfied, I will direct that my banners be sent to every stewardship, castlewick, and corporation."

These words greatly appeased the more moderate of the multitude, who said, "It is well: we wish for nothing more." The king, however, added yet further, "You, my good people of Kent, shall have one of my banners; and you also of Essex, Sussex, Bedford, Suffolk, Cambridge, Stafford, and Lincoln, shall each have one; I pardon you all for what you have hitherto done, but you must follow my banners and now return home on the terms I have mentioned," which they unanimously consented to do. Thus did this great assembly break up. The king instantly employed upwards of thirty secretaries, who drew up the letters as fast as they could, and when they were sealed and delivered to them, the people departed to their own counties. The principal mischief, however, remained behind: I mean Wat Tyler, Jack Straw, and John Ball, who declared, that though the people were satisfied, they were by no means so, and with them were about 30,000 also of the same mind. These all continued in the city without any wish to receive the letters or the king's seal, but did all they could to throw the town into such confusion, that the lords and rich citizens might be murdered and their houses pillaged and destroyed. The Londoners suspected this, and kept themselves at home, well armed and prepared to defend their property.

After he had appeased the people at Mile-end Green, King Richard went to the Wardrobe, in order that he might console the princess, who was in the greatest possible alarm. But I must not omit to relate an adventure which happened to these clowns before Norwich and to their leader, William Lister, who was from the county of Stafford. At the same time that a party of these wicked people in London burnt the palace of the Savoy, the church and house of St. John's, and the hospital of the Templars, there were collected numerous bodies of men from Lincolnshire, Norfolk, and Suffolk, who, according to the orders they had received, were marching towards London. On their road they stopped near Norwich, and forced every one whom they met to join them.

The reason of their stopping near Norwich was, that the governor of the town was a knight, by name Sir Robert Salle, who was not by birth a gentleman; but who, because of his ability and courage, had been created a knight by King Edward: he was, moreover, one of the handsomest and strongest men in England. Lister and his companions took it into their heads that they would make this man their commander. They, therefore, sent orders to him to come out into the fields to speak with them, declaring, in case he refused, that they would attack and burn the city. The knight, considering it was much better for him to go to them than that they should commit such outrages, mounted his horse and went out of the town alone to hear what they had to say. On his approach they showed every mark of respect, and courteously entreated him to dismount and talk with them. He did dismount, and in so doing committed a great folly, for immediately the mob surrounded him, and at first conversed in a friendly way, saying, "Robert, you are a knight and a man of great weight in this country, renowned for your valour; yet, notwithstanding all this, we know who you are; you are not a gentleman, but the son of a poor mason, such as ourselves. Come with us, therefore, as our commander, and we will make you so great a man that one quarter of England shall be under your control."

The knight, on hearing them speak thus, was exceedingly enraged, and eyeing them with angry looks said, "Begone, scoundrels and false traitors, would you have me desert my natural lord for such a company of knaves as you are? Would you have me dishonour myself? I would rather have you all hanged, for that must be your end." On saying this, he attempted to mount his horse; but his foot slipping from the stirrup, the animal took fright, and the mob upon this cried out, "Put him to death." Upon hearing which, Sir Robert let go his horse, and drawing a handsome Bordeaux sword, began to skirmish, and soon cleared the crowd from about him in an admirable manner. Many attempted to close with him; but each stroke he gave cut off heads, arms, feet, or legs, so that the boldest became afraid to approach him. The wretches were 40,000 in number, and he killed twelve of them and wounded many before they overpowered him, which at last they did with their missiles; and as soon as he was down, they cut off his arms and legs and rent his body piecemeal. Such was the pitiable end of Sir Robert Salle.

On Saturday morning the king left the Wardrobe and went to Westminster, when he and his lords heard mass in the abbey. In this church there is a statue of our Lady, in which the kings of England have much faith. To this on the present occasion King Richard and his nobles paid their devotions and made their offerings; they then rode in company along the causeway to London; but when they had proceeded a short distance, King Richard, with a few attendants, turned up a road on the left to go away from the city.

This day all the rabble again assembled under Wat Tyler, Jack Straw, and John Ball, at a place called Smithfield, where every Friday the horsemarket is kept. There were present about 20,000, and many more were in the city, breakfasting, and drinking Rhenish wine and Malmsey Madeira in the taverns and in the houses of the Lombards, without paying for anything; and happy was he who could give them good cheer to satisfy them. Those who collected in Smithfield had with them the king's banner, which had been given to them the preceding evening; and the wretches, notwithstanding this, wanted to pillage the city, their leaders saying, that hitherto they had done nothing. "The pardon which the king has granted will be of no use to us; but if we be of the same mind, we shall pillage this rich and powerful town of London before those from Essex, Suffolk, Cambridge, Bedford, Warwick, Reading, Lancashire, Arundel, Guildford, Coventry, Lynne, Lincoln, York, and Durham shall arrive; for they are on their road, and we know for certain that Vaquier and Lister will conduct them hither. Let us, then, be beforehand in plundering the wealth of the city; for if we wait for their arrival, they will wrest it from us." To this opinion all had agreed, when the king, attended by 60 horses, appeared in sight; he was at the time not thinking of the rabble, but had intended to continue his ride, without coming into London; however, when he arrived before the abbey of St. Bartholomew, which is in Smithfield, and saw the crowd of people, he stopped, saying that he would ascertain what they wanted, and endeavour to appease them. Wat Tyler, seeing the king and his party, said to his men, "Here is the king, I will go and speak with him; do you not stir until I give you a signal." He then made a motion with his hand, and added, "When you shall see me make this signal, then step forward, and kill every one except the king; but hurt him not, for he is young, and we can do what we please with him; carrying him with us through England, we shall be lords of the whole country, without any opposition." On saying which he spurred his horse and galloped up to the king, whom he approached so near that his horse's head touched the crupper of the king's horse.

His first words were these: "King, dost thou see all these men here?" "Yes," replied the king; "why dost thou ask?" "Because they are all under my command, and have sworn by their faith and loyalty to do whatsoever I shall order." "Very well," said the king: "I have no objection to it." Tyler, who was only desirous of a riot, made answer: "And thou thinkest, king, that these people, and as many more in the city, also under my command, ought to depart without having thy letters? No, indeed, we will carry them with us." "Why," replied the king, "it has been so ordered, and the letters will be delivered out one after another;

but, friend, return to thy companions, and tell them to depart from London; be peaceable and careful of yourselves; for it is our determination that you shall all have the letters by towns and villages according to our agreement." As the king finished speaking, Wat Tyler, casting his eyes round, spied a squire attached to the king's person bearing a sword. This squire Tyler mortally hated, and on seeing him, cried out, "What hast thou there? give me thy dagger." "I will not," said the squire: "why should I give it thee?" The king upon this said, "Give it to him; give it to him"; which the squire did, though much against his will. When Tyler took the dagger, he began to play with it in his hand, and again addressing the squire, said, "Give me that sword." "I will not," replied the squire, "for it is the king's sword, and thou being but a mechanic art not worthy to bear it; and if only thou and I were together, thou wouldst not have dared to say what thou hast, for a heap of gold as large as this church." "By my troth," answered Tyler, "I will not eat this day before I have thy head." At these words the Mayor of London, with about twelve men, rode forward, armed under their robes, and seeing Tyler's manner of behaving, said, "Scoundrel, how dare you to behave thus in the king's presence?" The king, also enraged at the fellow's impudence, said to the mayor, "Lay hands on him." Whilst King Richard was giving this order, Tyler still kept up the conversation, saying to the mayor: "What have you to do with it; does what I have said concern you?" "It does," replied the mayor, who found himself supported by the king, and then added: "I will not live a day unless you pay for your insolence." Upon saying which, he drew a kind of scimitar, and struck Tyler such a blow on the head as felled him to his horse's feet. As soon as the rebel was down, he was surrounded on all sides, in order that his own men might not see him; and one of the king's squires, by name John Standwich, immediately leaped from his horse, and drawing his sword, thrust it into his belly, so that he died.

When the rebels found that their leader was dead, they drew

up in a sort of battle array, each man having his bow bent before him. The king at this time certainly hazarded much, though it turned out most fortunately for him; for as soon as Tyler was on the ground, he left his attendants, giving orders that no one should follow him, and riding up to the rebels, who were advancing to revenge their leader's death, said, "Gentlemen, what are you about: you shall have me for your captain: I am your king, remain peaceable." The greater part, on hearing these words, were quite ashamed, and those among them who were inclined for peace began to slip away; the riotous ones, however, kept their ground. The king returned to his lords, and consulted with them what next should be done. Their advice was to make for the fields; but the mayor said, that to retreat would be of no avail. "It is quite proper to act as we have done; and I reckon we shall very soon receive assistance from our good friends in London."

While things were in this state, several persons ran to London, crying out, "They are killing the king and our mayor"; upon which alarm, all those of the king's party sallied out towards Smithfield, in number about seven or eight thousand. Among the first came Sir Robert Knolles and Sir Perducas d'Albret, well attended; then several aldermen, with upwards of 600 men-at-arms, and a powerful man of the city, by name Nicholas Bramber, the king's draper, bringing with him a large force on foot. These all drew up opposite to the rebels, who had with them the king's banner, and showed as if they intended to maintain their ground by offering combat.

The king created at this time three knights: Sir William Walworth, Sir John Standwich, and Sir Nicholas Bramber. As soon as Sir Robert Knolles arrived at Smithfield, his advice was immediately to fall upon the insurgents, and slay them; but King Richard would not consent to this. "You shall first go to them," he said, "and demand my banner; we shall then see how they will behave; for I am determined to have this by fair means or foul." The new knights were accordingly sent forward, and on approaching the rebels made signs to them not to shoot, as they wished to speak with them; and when within hearing, said, "Now attend; the king orders you to send back his banners; and if you do so, we trust he will have mercy upon you." The banners, upon this, were given up directly, and brought to the king. It was then ordered, under pain of death, that all those who had obtained the king's letters should deliver them up. Some did so, but not all; and the king on receiving them had them torn in pieces in their presence. You must know that from the time the king's banners were surrendered, these fellows kept no order; but the greater part, throwing their bows upon the ground, took to their heels and returned to London. Sir Robert Knolles was very angry that the rebels were not attacked at once and all slain; however, the king would not consent to it, saying, that he would have ample revenge without doing so.

When the rabble had dispersed, the king and his lords, to their great joy, returned in good array to London, whence the king immediately took the road to the Wardrobe, to visit the princess his mother, who had remained there two days and two nights under the greatest apprehension. On seeing her son, the good lady was much rejoiced, and said, "Ah, ah, fair son, what pain and anguish have I not suffered for you this day!" "Madam," replied the king, "I am well assured of that; but now rejoice, and thank God, for it behoves us to praise him, as I have this day regained my inheritance—the kingdom of England, which I had lost."

This whole day the king passed with his mother, and a proclamation was made through all the streets, that every person who was not an inhabitant of London, and who had not resided there for a whole year, should instantly depart; for if any of a contrary description were found in the city on Sunday morning at sunrise, they would be arrested as traitors to the king, and have their heads cut off. This proclamation no one dared to infringe, but all instantly departed to their homes quite discomfited.

John Ball and Jack Straw were found hidden in an old ruin,

where they had secreted themselves, thinking to steal away when things were quiet; but this they were prevented doing, for their own men betrayed them. With this capture the king and his barons were much pleased, and had their heads cut off, as was that of Tyler's, and fixed on London-bridge, in the room of those whom these wretches themselves had placed there.

News of this total defeat of the rebels in London was sent throughout the neighbouring counties, in order that all those who were on their way to London might hear of it; and as soon as they did so, they instantly returned to their homes, without daring to advance further. . . .

After the death of Tyler, Jack Straw, John Ball, and several others, the people being somewhat appeased, the king resolved to visit his bailiwicks, castlewicks, and stewardships, in order to punish the principal insurgents, and to recover the letters of pardon which had been forced from him, as well as to settle other matters tending to the peace of the realm. By a secret summons he assembled 500 spears and as many archers, and with them took the road to Kent, in which quarter the rebellion had first broken out. The first place he stopped at was a village called Comprinke; here he ordered the mayor, and all the men of the village, to be called, with whom one of his council remonstrated, telling them how much they had erred, and that because this mischief, which had nearly proved the ruin of England, must have had some advisers, it was better that the ringleaders should suffer than the whole; his majesty, therefore, demanded, under pain of incurring his displeasure for ever, that those should be pointed out who had been most culpable. When the people heard this, and saw that the innocent might escape by pointing out the guilty, they looked at each other, and said: "My lord, here is one by whom this town was excited." Immediately the person alluded to was taken and hanged, as were seven others. The letters-patent, which had been granted, were demanded back, and given up to the king's officer, who tore them in pieces, saying, "We command, in the king's name, all you who are here assembled to depart every one to his own home in peace; that you never more rebel against the king or against his ministers. By the punishment which has been inflicted your former deeds are pardoned." The people with one voice exclaimed, "God bless the king and his good council." In the same manner they acted in many other places in Kent, and, indeed, throughout England, so that upwards of 1,500 were beheaded or hanged; and it was not till all this was over, and everything quiet, that the king sent for the Duke of Lancaster from Scotland.

A Chronicle of Henry VI
(*ca. 1460*)

The political breakdown of the 1440s mentioned in the introduction to this chapter is illustrated in the following excerpts from *A Chronicle of Henry VI* and two brief selections from another chronicle, called the *Continuation of the Brut*.[20] Both were compiled about 1460-70, are strongly Yorkist in tone, and were derived largely from what are known as the "London Chronicles," succinct accounts of contemporary events kept by different city officials.[21] By the close of the 14th century the Latin monastic chronicle was giving way to its municipal counterpart. The 14th-century part of *The Brut* was written in French, but after 1400 most chroniclers employed English. The vernacular was rapidly emerging from the Middle English of Langland and Chaucer into the modern idiom. Nevertheless, 15th-century English is difficult for the uninitiated to read. Therefore, in the selection below a few obsolete words and expressions have been replaced and the spelling modernized. Otherwise the text remains unchanged, to preserve the flavor of the period. Incidentally, *A Chronicle of Henry VI* was among the first books printed in England by Caxton, about 1480.

DISINTEGRATION OF MEDIEVAL SOCIETY

The growth of Parliament in the 14th and early 15th centuries prepared the way eventually for a method of resolving political conflict by peaceful means. Yet the movement toward political stability was halting. Resort to force was almost endemic in medieval England. Of the nine kings who ruled England between the death of Edward I in 1307 and the accession of Henry VII in 1485, four were murdered (Edward II, Richard II, Henry VI, and Edward V) and another was killed in battle (Richard III). The incidence of violent death among the nobility ran even higher, especially during the Wars of the Roses. The events of 1447-50 narrated here prepared the way for that bloody struggle. During the early years of Henry VI's reign three men had dominated the English government: the king's two uncles, Humphrey, duke of Gloucester, and John, duke of Bedford, and their cousin Cardinal Henry Beaufort, bishop of Winchester. Although considerable rivalry existed, especially between Gloucester and Beaufort, England enjoyed relative stability until the 1430s. In 1429 the French began to rally under Joan of Arc; six years later Bedford, who had led the war effort, died in France. By 1447 the English were losing ground rapidly in France, Cardinal Beaufort had retired, and Gloucester's influence was waning. His chief rivals were Edmund Beaufort, duke of Somerset, and William de la Pole, duke of Suffolk, leaders of a faction which supported the unpopular queen, Margaret of Anjou. Whether true or not, the widespread belief that they murdered Gloucester demonstrates the loss of public trust. Gloucester's friends determined upon revenge. The politics of violence had begun again; it would last for half a century. Except possibly for Gloucester, every man mentioned in the following narrative (Beaumont, Buckingham, Fiennes, Gloucester, Shrewsbury, Somerset, and Suffolk) died by violence.[22]

A Chronicle of Henry VI

And in the month of February (1447) began the parliament at Saint Edmundsbury in Suffolk; the which parliament was made only for to slay the noble duke of Gloucester, whose death the false duke of Suffolk, William de la Pole, and Sir James Fiennes, lord Say, and others of their assent, had long time conspired and imagined. And they seeing that they might not slay him by any true means of justice nor any law, informed falsely the king, and said that he would raise the Welshmen for to distress the king and destroy him, and ordered that every lord should come to the said parliament in their best array and with strength. And all the ways about the said town of Bury, by commandment of the said Duke of Suffolk, were kept with great multitude of people of the country, waking day and night . . . and the weather was so cold that some of the poor people that were waked died for cold.

And towards the end of the parliament, the said duke of Gloucester was sent for, for to come and answer to such points of treason as should be laid against him; and ere he came fully into the town of Bury, there were sent unto him messengers commanding him on the king's behalf, that he should go straight to his inn, and come not nigh the king until he had otherwise in commandment. And the second day after, whilst he sat in the inn, came a sergeant of arms and arrested certain knights and squires and other special servants of his, and took them to divers prisons.

And the third day after, the lord Beaumont with others, that is to say, the duke of Buckingham, the duke of Somerset, and others, came to the said duke of Gloucester and arrested him: and then were certain of the king's house commanded to wait on him. And the third day after he died for sorrow, as some men said, because he might not come to his answer and excuse him of such things as were falsely put on him, for the said duke of Suffolk and lord Say, and others of their assent, so stirred and excited the king against the said duke of Gloucester that he might never come to his excuse. For they had cast among them a privy conclusion [conspiracy], the which as yet is not come to the knowledge of the common people, and they wist well that they should never bring it about until he were dead.

The next paragraph is taken from another chronicler, author of the continuation of the Brut.

But how he died, and in what manner, the certainty is not known to me. Some said he died for sorrow; some said he was murthered between two featherbeds; others said that an hot spit was put in his foundment [anus]. And so how he died God knoweth, to whom is no thing hid. And when he was thus dead, he was laid out, that all men might see him. And so both lords and knights of the shire with burgesses came and saw him dead; but they could not perceive wound nor token of how he died. Here may men mark what this world is! This duke was a noble man and a great clerk [scholar], and had worshipfully ruled this realm in the King's behalf and never could be found fault in him, but envy of them that were governors, and had promised the duchy of Anjou and the earldom of Maine. They caused the death of this noble man; for they dreaded, that he would prevent that surrender. . . . The death of this noble duke of Gloucester began the trouble in the realm of England and all the commons of the realm began to murmur for it, and were not content.

Returning to A Chronicle of Henry VI.

And this year on the Tuesday in Easterweek died master Harry Beaufort, bishop of Winchester and priest cardinal of Rome. . . .

The XXVIII year of King Henry [1449], the feast of St. Simon and St. Jude, and other days before and after, the sun in his rising and going down appeared as red as blood, as many men saw: whereof the people had great marvel, and deemed that it betokened some harm soon afterward.

And this same year, on the feast of St. Michael, Rouen was lost and yielded to the Frenchmen; being therein that time the duke of Somerset and earl of Shrewsbury. . . .

The XXIX year of King Henry, Normandy was lost by the untruth and false courtesy of Edmund duke of Somerset, being that time lieutenant of Normandy; for he menaced and abated the number of soldiers that were in the garrisons, and sent them into England unpaid of their wages, whereby the strength of Normandy was lost.

And the common view and fame was that time that the duke of Suffolk, William de la Pole, and the said duke of Somerset, with others of their assent, had made deliverance of Anjou and Maine without the assent of this land [England] unto the king of Sicily the queen's father; and had also alienated and sold the duchy of Normandy to the king of France; wherefore all the people of this land and especially the commons cried against the said duke of Suffolk, and said he was a traitor. And at the instance and petition of the said commons of the parliament holden that time at Westminster, he was arrested and put in the Tower.

This duke of Suffolk had asked before this time of one that was an astronomer [astrologer], what should befall him, and how he should end his life; and when the said astronomer had laboured therefore in his said craft, he answered to the duke and said that he should die a shameful death, and counseled him always to be ware of the Tower. Wherefore by instance of lords that were his friends, he was delivered out of the said Tower of London.

Then the king seeing that all this land hated the said duke deadly, and that he might not bear nor abide the malice of the people, exiled him for a term of five years. And the Friday the third day of May (1450), he took ship at Ipswich and sailed forth in to the high sea, where another ship called the *Nicholas of the Tower* lay in wait for him, and took him.[23] And they that were within granted him space of a day and a night to shrive him [for his confession to his chaplain, who was with him], and make him ready to God. And then a knave of Ireland smote off his head, upon the side of the boat of the said *Nicholas of the Tower*, notwithstanding his safe conduct; and the body with the head was cast to the land at Dover.

The author of the Brut tells substantially the same story, concluding with the following comments.

Lo! what availed him now all his deliverance of Normandy etc. And here ye may learn how he was rewarded for the death of the duke of Gloucester.

This began sorrow upon sorrow, and death for death.

NOTES TO CHAPTER V

1. M. M. Postan, ed., *The Cambridge Economic History*, vol. 1, *The Agrarian Life of the Middle Ages*, 2nd ed. (Cambridge: Cambridge University Press, 1966), pp. 566-70.
2. (London: Allen and Unwin, 1962; New York: Humanities Press, 1963). See also Eleanora Carus-Wilson and Olive Coleman, *England's Export Trade, 1275-1543* (New York: Oxford University Press, 1963).
3. *The Later Middle Ages, 1272-1485* (London: Nelson, 1962), pp. 29-30, 248.
4. "Lord Hastings' Indentured Retainers, 1461-83," *Transactions of the Connecticut Academy of Arts and Sciences* 39 (New Haven, 1955): 1-175.
5. *England under the Yorkists and the Tudors, 1471-1603* (London: G. Bell and Sons, 1968).
6. *Prejudice and Promise in Fifteenth Century England* (Oxford: Clarendon Press, 1925), p. 66. Quoted in part by E. F. Jacob, *The Fifteenth Century, 1399-1485* (Oxford: Clarendon Press, 1961), p. v. Yet old values died slowly. The paradox of the age is illustrated by the fact that a businessman like William Caxton, a Merchant Adventurer and England's first printer, strongly "exhorted the English aristocracy to renew their dedication to the principles and practices of chivalry." Arthur B. Ferguson, *The Indian Summer of English Chivalry* (Durham, N.C.: Duke University Press, 1960), p. 34.
7. (Thou mayest say) "I'm a King, I'm a Prince!"
But thou mayest perhaps be neither hereafter;
O thou that dost administer the special laws of king Christ,
That thou mayest do this the better, be merciful as thou art just.
Naked justice needs to be clothed by thee in mercy.
Such harvest as thou wouldest reap, such the seeds thou shouldest sow.
If thou strip justice naked, mayest thou meet with naked justice;
If thou hast sown mercy, mayest thou reap mercy!

8. Since a king may be said to take his name from the act of ruling, He has the name without the reality, unless he studies to keep the laws.

9. The king's commandments are the chains of law to us.

10. Woe to the land where a boy is king.

11. From penalty and guilt.

12. Let you salute no one on the way.

13. And those who do good shall go into eternal life, But those who do evil into eternal fire.

14. Though I walk in the valley of the shadow of death, I will fear no evil, for Thou art with me.

15. Be not anxious.

16. He spoke foolishly.

17. Whatever thou shalt bind on earth shall be bound in heaven.

18. Anthony Steel, *Richard II* (Cambridge: Cambridge University Press, 1962), p. 50.

19. Simon Sudbury, archbishop of Canterbury and chancellor, was a politically minded bishop attached to John of Gaunt's party. He had imprisoned John Ball. Note how the activities of the rebels reveal both an anti-clericalism and a strong prejudice against foreigners such as the Flemings.

20. *An English Chronicle of the Reigns of Richard II, Henry IV, Henry V and Henry VI*, ed. Rev. John Silvester Daivies, Camden Society, vol. 64 (London, 1856), pp. 62-63, 68-69. *The Brut or the Chronicles of England*, pt. 2, ed. Friedrich W. D. Brie (London: Kegan Paul, Trench, Truebner & Co., 1908), pp. 512-13, 516.

21. C. L. Kingsford, *English Historical Literature in the Fifteenth Century* (London: Oxford University Press, 1913), p. 121.

22. Lord John Beaumont and Humphrey Stafford, duke of Buckingham, were both killed at the battle of Northampton in 1460. Sir James Fiennes, Lord Say, was assassinated during Cade's rebellion in 1450. John Talbot, earl of Shrewsbury, died in the last battle against the French in Gascony in 1453. Edmund Beaufort, duke of Somerset, was killed at the first battle of Saint Albans in 1455. Even the astrologer mentioned, whose name appears to have been Stacey, was executed in 1477 for supporting "false fleeting Clarence" against King Edward IV. The author of the most recent general history of the 15th century believes that Gloucester was not murdered but suffered a stroke and died after being in a coma for three days. Jacob, *The Fifteenth Century, 1399-1485*, p. 483.

23. According to a letter written from London, 5 May 1450, Suffolk asked the name of the ship when he was taken aboard. When he learned that it was the *Nicholas of the Tower*, he recalled the prophecy of the astrologer that "if he might escape the danger of the *Tower* he should be safe, and then his heart failed him." *The Paston Letters, 1422-1509*, ed. James Gairdner, 4 vols. (Edinburgh: John Grant, 1910), 1:125.